POLYCHROMATIC ASSEMBLY FOR WOODTURNING

EMMETT BROWN

CYRIL BROWN

Edited by R. Sorsky

With an Introduction by Frank Knox

Fresno California

LINDEN PUBLISHING CO.

1982

POLYCHROMATIC ASSEMBLY FOR WOOD TURNING

Second Edition   Revised and Enlarged

Copyright © 1982 by Linden Publishing Co.

Originally Published by The Society of Ornamental Turners, England

468975

ISBN 0-941936-05-8

LINDEN PUBLISHING CO.
3845 North Blackstone
Fresno, California 93726

Cover illustration: Salad Bowl by Howard Oldaker

TABLE OF CONTENTS

LIST OF ILLUSTRATIONS

ACKNOWLEDGEMENTS

In the extended process of gathering pictures and detailed information about the creations and methods of other craftsmen engaged in this type of woodwork it was inevitable that we became indebted to many who went to considerable labor and expense to support and expand the original scope of our monograph. As we now acknowledge their assistance and that of all who contributed in any way to its publication we wish to specifically thank friends whose craftwork appears in the Plates, without which, visual confirmation of the possibilities of the craft would be less attractive and convincing.

A. L. BRASELL	Wanganui, New Zealand	I.W.C.S.
R. C. GREENWALD	Florida, U.S.A.	I.W.C.S.
C. HOFFMAN	Pennsylvania, U.S.A.	I.W.C.S. &S.O.T.
M. M. KLINE	New York, U.S.A.	I.W.C.S. late S.O.T.
J.A. LARRALDE	California, U.S.A.	I.W.C.S. (Past President)
W. J. OSBORNE	Stratford-upon-Avon, England	S.O.T. Editor

We also feel that special mention should be made of the service rendered by Mr. Larralde whose unique wooden reproductions of Grecian ceramics are shown in Plates 31-33 and for the photographic aid given by Mr. C. A. Strakis of the Handsworth Photographic Society who spent many tedious hours producing plates of the smaller articles and equipment.

Emmett E. Brown
California,
U.S.A.

Cyril Brown
Birmingham,
England

ACKNOWLEDGEMENTS TO SECOND EDITION

Many people are responsible for the second edition of POLYCHROMATIC ASSEMBLY FOR WOOD TURNING. My special thanks are extended to Mr. Cyril Brown of England and to Mr. Emmett Brown of California for their permission to reprint this valuable monograph which deals with a field of wood turning upon which so little has been written. To my knowledge this is the first work published since 1916 which deals specifically with polychromatic assembly. Mr. Cyril Brown, a past Vice President of the International Wood Collectors Society, is the last surviving member to receive their Fellowship for special services to the membership. Cyril Brown is also a long time member of the Society of Ornamental Turners in England.

Mr. Emmett Brown, the co-author of POLYCHROMATIC ASSEMBLY FOR WOOD TURNING, did much of the pioneer practical work which is represented in the monograph. Mr. Brown was also for many years an active member of the International Wood Collectors Society and the Society of Ornamental Turners in England.

I am deeply indebted to Mr. Steven Goddard and to Mr. John Cammarata PE, CMC. Without the help, advice and long hours of work from these two men, this project would not have been possible. Their respective work on the bibliography and index will serve to make the monograph extremely useful for the reader. Both gentlemen were also instrumental in obtaining many of the photographs of current work being done in the field of polychromatic assembly.

Thanks are also due to Mr. Frank Knox for his fine introduction and to the following people who were kind enough to send photographs of their work. Miss Janice Cole, Mr. Paul Darnell, Mr. Thomas Duffy, Mr. Peter Higbee, Mr. Richard Schneider, Mr. Thomas Nicosia, Mr. Howard Oldaker, Mr. John Roccanova, Mr. Frank Knox, Mr. William Kravarik, Mr. John Millen, Mr. Michael Roccanova, Mr. John Barklow, and Mr. Cyril Brown.

R. Sorsky
Fresno
California
May 1982

PREFACE

In presenting this monograph we hope that the reader has some practical experience in plain wood turning by hand and some knowledge of the few machines, tools, workshop terms and operations to which we refer.

The decision to pool, rationalize, and then record in print our knowledge of polychromatic assembly and the associated craftwork was made during a meeting in Birmingham, England after ten years of correspondence, exchange of drawings photographs, specimens of typical assemblies and completed turnery.

Previously we had dealt with requests from other craftsmen seeking information about our methods, by means of taped letters and photographs which usually concerned elementary forms of assembly required for specified items of turnery. This was the easiest way to pass on limited explanations but cumulatively over the years it became expensive, repetitive, time consuming and occasionally confusing as we were not always in step or accord with changing and improving techniques.

Unfortunately, domestic circumstances reduced the time we could devote to further experimental assemblies and we realized that unless our findings were soon recorded they would not be available to others before the desire to do this had passed the limits of reliable memory preserved by regular performance.

Our text is restricted to a review of the polychromatic field as we know it together with brief descriptions of the methods and equipment we employed to produce the supporting range of wooden articles which follow. Apart from rotation, we regard wood turning as a manual craft, exercised by persons whom we believe will learn more from our drawings and photographs than an abundance of works. . . . and we prefer our exposition to be evaluated from the visual evidence provided.

Emmett Brown
California
U.S.A.
1973

Cyril Brown
Birmingham
England
1973

PREFACE TO THE SECOND EDITION

POLYCHROMATIC ASSEMBLY FOR WOOD TURNING was originally published in 1973 in a limited edition for the use of members of the Society of Ornamental Turners in England and for the membership of the International Society of Wood Collectors, based in the United States. The authors, Cyril Brown of England, and Emmett Brown of the United States, are both recognized masters of the art and developed many of the procedures used in the craft today. Both men were deeply involved in turning and introduced many people to this form of lathe work. The original work was approximately five years in the making and involved a considerable amount of international correspondence not only between the Browns but also with many other turners worldwide.

Polychromatic assembly is one of the most difficult, yet rewarding forms of woodturning currently being practiced. The skills required are really the focus of all skills required in general woodworking. There is, however little room for error of any type if the finished product is to merit the necessary time expended upon it. Yet this should not deter the novice turner because the results of this form of turning can be astounding. The enjoyment of working with rare and beautiful woods in combination reaches its ultimate in polychromatic assembly. Nowhere does nature's art combine with man's skill and inventiveness as it does in this decorative form of turning.

This is the only book dealing extensively with polychromatic assembly to be written in the last 66 years and it is the hope of both authors that this second edition will serve to advance and expand interest in a craft which becomes more essential as a decorative and production medium as wood supplies become more limited, expensive and difficult to obtain.

R. Sorsky
Fresno, California
U.S.A.
1982

INTRODUCTION

Woodworking as a hobby has few equals in its appeal to both men and women of all ages in life. In recent years it has been explosive in its growth and is now fully established as a number one leisure time occupation for many, both as a hobby and as a profession.

Whether it is followed as a profession of cabinet making, as the refinishing of antique furniture, or as exercises on the turning lathe, either plain or ornamental, it has gathered more followers than almost any other activity. For the rapidly growing number of senior citizens it comes as manna from heaven as a challenge to long neglected creativity and as a means of putting leisure time to productive use.

Books on the subject have become legion and more and more schools are teaching it in one form or another. What can be more gratifying than a bud vase from a turning lathe, a kite that flies for the youngster or grandma's old rocking chair restored to use? It is only natural that new and more exciting applications should be sought as one progresses and one such application is to be found in what is known a polychromatic assembly for wood turning, and that is the subject of this book.

Wood is, in itself, one of nature's most exciting and wonderful products. The varieties in color and grain pattern offer man one of the most exacting and productive areas of creative effort in producing beautiful objects of art as well as useful products. Polychromatic assembly greatly extends the possibilities for exciting patterns by taking advantage of the blending and combinations of these colors and grain patterns to produce effects which are on the one hand lovely to look at and on the other puzzling in their bizarre effect. When combined with the turning lathe really wonderful effects are obtained which are a challenge to the amateur and professional alike.

It has been said that, in working with wood, there are only four factors to be considered; measuring, marking, cutting and joining. At the risk of over simplification the beginner soon learns the truth of this statement. Polychromatic assembly and turnery brings these four into sharp focus as no other form of woodworking with the possible exception of ornamental turnery. The detailed instructions and illustrations furnished here provide the amateur with professional guidance, given by those who have become masters of the art. They will guide him away from many of the mistakes which otherwise might have been made.

If the woodworker will learn to master the above four factors of measuring, marking, cutting and joining and will select woods of pleasing color and grain pattern he will open the door to some of the most exciting and pleasing results of this miracle of nature's handicraft - wood. It is a challenge to the creative ability of the amateur as well as the professional woodworker. This book tells how to do that.

FRANK M. KNOX
New York, N.Y.
1982

PLATE I

POLYCHROMATIC ASSEMBLY FOR WOOD TURNING

PRINCIPAL FORMS				PRODUCTION METHODS	TYPICAL UTILIZATION
	TYPE	EXAMPLE	CHARACTER		
STUDDING	SIMPLE		Projecting or flush insertions into flat or cylindrical surfaces in form of circular studs, cores or discs.	Turned, sawn, punched or cut by hollow drill, glued and then over-drilled for compound patterns.	Decoration on lids, cylindrical boxes, dishes, mirror & picture frames, plinths, trophy mounts.
	COMPOUND				
BLOCKING — SINGLE TIER	RECT-ANGULAR		Flat, shallow, chequered stock.	Circular sawn in strips, glued, cramped and operations repeated in varying angles, combinations and patterns.	Chess & draught boards, centres for trays & tables.
	CHEVRON		Flat, shallow, chevron stock.		Plaques, plates, dishes, trays, salvers, bases, buttons, medallions, wood jewellery & mounts.
	COMPOUND		Flat, shallow stock in geometrical patterns.		
	ABSTRACT		Flat, shallow stock in irregular, random patterns.		
BLOCKING — MULTI-TIER	SPINDLE		Square stock in rectangular patterns.	Circular sawn, glued & cramped.	Candlestick & lamp stems, shakers, Tunbridge stickware.
	DISC		Flat stock in layers of rectangular patterns.		Fruit, nut, salad and other bowls, deep trays, boxes, lamp bases, mirror and picture frames.
SEGMENTING — RING	FLAT		Edging & other thick decorative bands, overlaid or inlaid.	Circular sawn in sliding mitre gauge, glued & cramped by circular band.	
	CYLINDER		Hollow, deep cylindrical stock.	Circular sawn by inclination, glued & cramped by circular bands.	Biscuit barrels, tobacco holders, drinking vessels, napkin rings.
SEGMENTING — SECTOR	STRAIGHT		Flat, shallow stock in geometrical patterns.	Circular sawn in sliding mitre gauge, glued & cramped by circular band.	Plaques, plates, dishes, trays, salvers, plinths, buttons, vases.
	SHAPED			Band or jigsawn, glued, cramped by circular band.	

ASSEMBLY METHODS AND EQUIPMENT

It is anyone's guess how, why and when assemblies of multicolored and varied shapes of wood first became associated with fine woodwork. Its particular application to turnery eventually became accepted as a distinct form of the craft. Maybe it was an economical desire to produce more stock from remnants of elegant, well-seasoned timber, an experimental attempt to add variety to the patterns not encountered in natural wood formations.

Certainly segmented assemblies for wheels, barrels and other utility articles in circular forms used for many generations, were the outcome of limitations in material size and strength. Later, these principles of assembly were applied to more decorative constructions.

The terminology that had been used to define various forms of polychromatic work we considered inconsistent, ambiguous and often misleading so we prepared a chart to explain by text and illustration specific meanings for the terms used in this monograph which may not accord with strict literal definitions. (PLATE 1).

It should also be understood that only simple examples of polychromatic assembly are presented, and the methods described are those used by a few experienced craftsmen in our circle of acquaintance. Many alternative ways for producing very similar assemblies have been employed and the only claim we make is that ours gives satisfactory results.

With the exception of Ornamental Turnery, we do not know any other form of wood decoration which calls for greater mechanical precision and improvisation of equipment to produce top quality articles, than polychromatic assembly. This can be an inexpensive means for producing suitable stock for fine turnery or very costly when the initial whim develops into a compulsive urge to employ a wide range of natural wood colors in dimensions beyond those normally extracted from stock used for small plates, bowls, buttons and wood jewelry.

Books and articles on polychromatic turnery published in the early years of this century suggest that most of the operations connected with studding and segmentation were performed with hand tools because precision woodworking machinery was not then available in the modestly priced units now owned by many enthusiastic wood hobbyists. This implies that the advent of the drill press, dimensional sawbench and lathe with indexed headstock and sliderest has made it possible to obtain a high degree of accuracy so essential for this type of woodwork without need of advanced manual skill. Our monograph assumes that such machinery is available and that the craftsman is able to construct the other simple equipment described, from materials usually offered in small lots from local hardware stores and metal stockists.

Detailed drawings of typical polychromatic assemblies converted into successful projects, showing their colors, proportions, wood cutting schedules etc. accompany this monograph. The purpose of this monograph is however, to explain the mechanical rather than the artistic approach to the craft as good appearance depends so much upon individual taste, design ability and a supply of suitable timber at acceptable cost.

The usual applications of polychromatic work are for (1) Adding decoration to simple turnery forms such as plates, salvers, mirror and picture frames, box lids etc. by means of studding, centerpieces, plain and segmented rings as inlays, overlays or edgings. (2) Production of variegated stock for complete disc or spindle turnery. (3) Production of blended stock assemblies which fully utilize expensive timber, improve the stability of the turnery and provide stock in dimensions not generally available at moderate cost.

The principal forms of polychromatic assembly which we have charted are sometimes used in combination but more often as separate decorative mediums. Studding is exclusively a surface decoration whereas Blocking can be employed for many types of faceplate or spindle turnery. Segmenting is usually restricted to disc and cylindrical work.

STUDDING is a form of decoration which has more substance than marquetry, achieved by the insertion of shallow circular discs or cross sections of cylinders into the body of an article. Studs usually finish flush or slightly above the general surface level of the work. They may be of a single or several contrasting woods or of polychromatic assembly, the last mentioned is a rewarding way of utilizing small offcuts of this kind of stock. Studs are usually made on a lathe but can be produced more rapidly but less satisfactorily by hollow cutting tools on the drill press or crosscut from commercial dowels or self turned cylinders.

Effective decorative patterns can be obtained by means of simple studding and major ornamentation by compound arrangements in greater variety of woods. These can be in the form of concentric rings of overlapped insertions by multiple operations, geometric in character.

Studding is a decorative medium particularly suitable for execution by an ornamental turning lathe. The ornamental turning lathe has an indexed headstock, eccentric chuck, calibrated sliderest and special cutting frames which make the operation of rabbeting and shaping discs a simple mechanical repetition. Even so, satisfactory results can be achieved by careful manual setting out and the use of flat bottomed tools in the drill press.

Studs should not fit too tightly in their rabbets as a distinct glueline helps to accentuate the contrast between woods and a tolerance allows surplus adhesive to escape. They should always be given slightly concave bottoms or shoulders to ensure firm, uniform seating and when of considerable diameter, a slight taper towards their base facilitates the insertion, avoids distortion and risk of splitting the article being decorated.

Studs which are required to finish flush with the general surface of an article should project a little after insertion and then be pared down with a very sharp chisel and skimmed level with a turning tool. Great care must be observed to avoid the splintering of edges. If this occurs an uneven local surface will appear which is likely to be aggravated rather than rectified by severe abrasive treatment. If studs are to remain proud of the general surface they should be completed, including polishing before insertion and they seat and look better when turned with heads that overlap their stems.

Small studs can usually be settled in position by light hammer taps over a covering block to eliminate bruising, splitting or the glancing blow that can damage the major article. Large studs may need a more regulated force to seat them snugly such as pressure applied by clamp or vise. An old letter press can be employed for this purpose. A covering disc with a turned reverse profile should be used if the studs have shaped heads. It is assumed that a competent turner will devise methods for producing identical studs in the quantities desired.

Finally a note of caution regarding the choice of woods for studs, particularly when their heads reveal direct end grain. Use tough close grained, plain wood species and remember that considerable differences of hue occur between untreated and polished components which can upset a color scheme and cause much disappointment.

PLATE 7 shows a typical application of simple studding and some interesting compound patterns we have successfully inserted in a variety of flat and cylindrical surfaces.

BLOCKING is an assembly of small blocks of wood in regular or random patterns. They may be single, multiple or interlocked tiers which are converted into principal or secondary decorations for turned articles. In addition they may be stock in which the block pattern serves in place of the overall figuring of an ordinary wood growth.

Most of our advanced blocking patterns have been developed in single tiers to furnish stock for a range of shallow section turnery or as centerpieces of larger projects in which the greater part of the assembly is utilized and viewed in one plane. Multiple tier and spindle constructions can be very wasteful in materials and of uncertain strength unless carefully designed to ensure that pleasing external appearance is linked with a sound arrangement of interlocking blocks, not an easy exercise when contours and diameters of finished work vary considerably.

The customary way to obtain a strip of wood for blocking from a saw bench is to set the rip fence off the adjacent parallel saw face plus an allowance for the set of the teeth and then feed the stock steadily into and past the revolving saw with enough lateral pressure to maintain unbroken contact with the ripfence. This method can produce strips to close limits but sometimes with the sawn face scored by the teeth and scorched if the wood is cross grained, knotty, resinous, warped or badly fed into the machine.

An extra width of strip is required to accommodate the planing or sanding of sawn edges, both detrimental to an adhesive bond since planing hardens the surface of the wood and sanding clogs its pores. The strongest glue joints are obtained from strips used straight from the saw, especially when produced by hollow-ground planer or combination blades which we recommend for top quality work.

Satisfactory results can be obtained from standard rip saws 10" in diameter of 16-18 gauge with around 50 teeth given a fairly fine set on their tips which can be sharpened and reset while remaining on the saw spindle. It is essential to keep the saw sharp and running true at all times, otherwise strips will not be accurate enough for assembly straight from the sawbench. The use of cross cut saws may have advantages for certain transverse cuts on partly assembled stock (influenced by the character of the woods involved). Gluelines usually check splintering also, a loose backing strip in the miter gauge, which is cut to waste, restrains end and edge fractures on stock prone to shattering when being cross cut.

The method we have adopted to minimize saw wobbles, wood binding and fence friction is by means of a sliding carrier which traverses in the lefthand miter gauge groove of the sawbench and a hinged fence attached to the rip fence which is folded back during the sawing operation. (PLATES 2 & 3)

To obtain a strip of given width the hinged fence is positioned via the rip fence for a normal ripping act. The sliding carrier is then located in the miter gauge groove just forward of the emergent saw and the stock moved laterally to bear upon the face of the hinged fence. The carrier bar thumbscrews are adjusted so that their dome ends clamp the stock firmly down on the wood lined surface of the carrier and then the hinged fence is turned over to its neutral position. The desired strip can now be obtained by advancing the loaded carrier to and past the revolving saw, repeating the setting of stock and fence for each additional strip. A trial strip of narrow width should be taken to true the edge of the stock before the first work strip is sawn. Provided the saw is sharp, running true and the carrier moving smoothly in the groove without lateral play, clean saw cuts giving perfectly matched strips should be obtained. We have no difficulty in producing them in a width of 1/60", length being limited by that of the carrier and depth by the exposed saw, convenient maximum dimensions being 24" and 1" respectively.

Angular cuts on plain stock or glued assemblies to produce strips for opposed grain, checkered, chevron or abstract pattern assemblies are usually commenced in the sliding miter gauge and may then be transferred to the sliding carrier which can be fitted with a miter bar to give extra support to the carrier bar thumbscrews. The hinged fence is used to determine the width of the strips.

The other essential requirement for polychromatic assembly is sound clamping technique. For the simple, occasional project it is possible to mangage with sash, G, C, and other workshop clamping devices but we strongly advise the ambitious craftsman to make a few blocking presses which employ the principles of the Universal Press shown in PLATE 6 and the supporting description. In return for a modest capital outlay, equipment can be constructed that will give superior results, take less time and leave the ordinary accessories free for emergencies.

The quantity, range and dimensions of presses should be related to the patterns required, the number of assemblies in mind over a known period and the capacity of the sawbench available. Unless you have unlimited time and patience in which to assemble the stages of a complicated design, we suggest that a minimum of three presses is a sensible number to make, otherwise it might be more convenient to settle for one universal type.

During assembly, care must be taken to regulate the compression so that it is firmly and evenly, but not excessively, applied over the full extent of the gluelines, remembering that it is the conduct of the softest wood used which is most likely to affect the accuracy of the construction and determine the final degree of pressure. Excessive pressure at any point tends to alter the width of the assembly and distort the gluelines in vertical and horizontal directions which causes bad registration of logical meeting points in subsequent secondary assemblies.

Commercial veneers are useful to provide thin strips to accentuate contrasts between wider strips and wood species, to delineate sectors of segmentations, or as laminae in tiered assemblies. Although expensive in terms of wood volume, when judiciously incorporated, veneers reduce the number of boards required and extend the range of species likely to be encountered by hobby woodworkers with limited timber yard contacts. We use veneers of 1/60" and 1/30" thickness and slit them by knife or fine saw. Small quantities of very choice veneers are sawn from the block or plank in the sliding carrier.

SINGLE TIER BLOCKING is usually less than 1" thick and used chiefly as a surface decoration for shallow section turnery. It provides the widest scope for variety in patterns and color combinations ranging from vivid contrasts to restrained harmonies and can be regarded as the easiest form of assembly in which to gain experience in this class of work. A project may be wholly composed of polychromatic blocks, receive them as an overlay or inlay or enclose them within a framework of plain stock. Where the polychromatic work serves as a simple decorative feature of the main article, the matrix wood is often figured but when it covers most of a prominent surface the surrounding wood should be of a plain character.

Curious craftsmen will soon develop their own patterns, in the main variations of the four types depicted in PLATE 1. Of these the Rectangular form is the most common and easiest to produce, a familiar example being the two color checkers used for game boards with squares larger than the width of strips usually preferred for decorative assemblies. This pattern is obtained by an initial assembly of alternate contrasting strips which are cross-sawn into checkered strips then reassembled into an overall checkered square.

The Chevron pattern is produced by a similar routine except that the first strip assembly is directed to the saw in the miter gauge at an angle of 45° for the cross-sawing operation. The resulting chevron strips are alternately reversed in the second assembly which yields rather large offcuts if converted into a disc. Fortunately, most of them can be used for smaller items or embodied in abstract assemblies. We are very partial to chevron pattern blocking which has furnished some of our most striking and successful patterns having an affinity with Navajo and other traditional Indian decorative motifs. These have been used as the principal decoration for large plates and as the entire stock for small salvers, plaques and collectors buttons. (PLATES 8 & 10)

COMPOUND patterns are geometrical strip combinations of rectangular and chevron types of blocking which can be comfortably assembled in the kind of press shown in PLATE 5.

ABSTRACT patterns are usually composed of the many off cuts from other types of single tier blocking. To facilitate assembly the anchor bars of the blocking press are given angular locations and shaped packs are used to obtain tight glue lines, a piecemeal process that is slow and sometimes tedious. It is good practice to enclose abstract assemblies with wide margins of solid stock and as far as possible avoid pattern gluelines which meet or approach perimeters in a near tangential manner. This precaution will reduce flaking and surface fracture of joints during lathe operations.

MULTI-TIER BLOCKING in spindle form has long been accepted as an economical method of building up stock for turnery of large diameter, often with a core of stronger or cheaper wood that will not be exposed. In decorative form it has chiefly been regarded as a novelty, a typical example being Tunbridge stickware of the last century. The use of a core simplifies the construction of stock and reduces the risk of collapse on the lathe from glueline faults and inadequate interlocking of components. It also assists in the assessment of patterns likely to emerge from experimental assemblies and ensures symmetry when the surrounding blocks are accurately sawn and suitably arranged. PLATE 1 shows a simple assembly with uniform cross-section, but considerable variations in spindle diameter and pattern can be accommodated by progressive addition of smaller blocks to the major components around the core, preferably determined with the help of a scale drawing. Longitudinal laminations added to the whole or greater part of a rectangular core are a form of assembly from which a twice revealed pattern can be obtained, perhaps not quite as pleasing as the quadruplicate effect of the fully balanced four side additions. PLATES 9 & 11 give some examples.

DISC stock is usually built up from single tier assemblies with meeting surfaces made true by planing and sanding. Great care must be taken to ensure that vertical block lines are correctly positioned when the glued tiers are assembled under moderate compression. Stock up to 12" square can be satisfactorily assembled in an old letter press supplemented by a few "C" or "G" clamps. Beyond this size you will probably have to devise a special press. Perfectly sound and elegant bowls and other shallow section turnery can be produced from assemblies of rectangular blocks but it is more economical and satisfactory craftwise when segmentation is adopted for deep hollow turnery.

SEGMENTING is the most exacting type of polychromatic assembly which requires angular sawing directed by the mitergauge on a level top sawbench against the ripfence of a tilting spindle, or canting table sawbench or by template for shaped cuts on band or jigsaw. It is essential to prepare full size drawings of segmented projects so that the most suitable number of segments, pattern colors and dimensions are determined before any machine work is commenced, otherwise a lot of material and time will be wasted.

RING flats are normally assembled from segments cut from flat strips. They can also be sawn from sections of ring cylinders described later. The drawing is commenced by scribing the pitch circle of the required ring, followed by inner and outer circles to contain the segmented blank with ample allowance for turning trim. The number of segments is then settled, bearing in mind that their outer edges are straight lines (chords) which make end point contact with the band clamp during assembly, so long chord lengths are to be avoided. Segments which incline to square proportions give the best results. We prefer a segment total of not less than 15 and often raise this to 60 for large diameter rings. If the total is a multiple of 360 it is conducive to easy setting out with a standard protractor. The final divisions should be checked with dividers and the sector line extended to a circle large enough to contain the miter gauge in order to make a more precise setting of its usually coarse angular scale. Within rational limits, the larger the setting-out circle the greater the accuracy likely to be secured for segment division and thus the miter gauge setting, in combination with major chord dimensions, controls the accuracy of the segment delivered by the sawbench.

The exact angles and dimensions for all components of any segment ring can be easily calculated but are seldom located on coarse machine scales with out trial and error runs using waste strips of wood, ply or hardboard. The important thing to obtain is a miter gauge setting that will deliver a segment ring perfectly closed by the selected number of segments and from which an identical segment template can be made. A slight discrepancy in the length of the major chord reflects sharply in the size of the complete assembly and, if this is critical in the design of a project, dummy runs must continue until the settings of the segment template and the segment stop produce the dimensions required.

Whether the initial miter gauge setting is taken from the drawing or calculation we strongly advise the purchase or construction of gauges which can be given permanent settings for all circle divisions in regular demand. They can be made cheaply from oddments of wood, ply, metal and machine screws in the form suggested on PLATE 5.

The segment sector angle is computed by dividing 360° by the total number of segments and half of this angular value is used to set the miter gauge to what we term the segment angle.

EXAMPLE: $\dfrac{360°}{36 \text{ segments}}$ = 10° (the sector angle)

$\dfrac{10°}{2}$ = 5° (the segment angle)

The length of the major segment chord is computed by multiplying it radius by the sine of the segment angle; the result is then doubled.

EXAMPLE:
6.6" (the radius) X 0.0872 (the sine of 5°) X 2 = 1.15" (about 1 5/32").

The segment template can be made from a flat piece of ½" thick plywood with parallel sides, one of which is held against the fence of the miter gauge set at the segment angle. The plywood is traversed past the running saw to remove a triangular slice, then reversed laterally and a second slice is removed to leave a template with side angles similar to those of the required segment. A strut is fixed at right angles and flush with the surface and one side edge for attachment to the ripfence by temporary screws or clamps.

The procedure to secure a segment is as follows; Hold the workstrip firmly against the miter gauge fence set to the segment angle and traverse past the running saw to obtain one side of the segment. Retract the gauge and reverse the strip by a half rotation and mark the length of the major chord on the forward edge from the sawn side, preferabley with vernier calipers. Align the chord and if correct clamp the strip to the miter gauge fence with stopped saw blade engaged in the kerf, then pull the loaded gauge back to leave a gap of about 2". Fix the segment template to the ripfence so that its most forward corner is a little nearer the saw than the workstrip and adjust the lateral position of the ripfence so that the free side edge of the template engages with the matching side edge of the workstrip. Insert the segment stop in the miter gauge groove immediately behind the gauge slidebar and the sawing set-up is ready, as indicated on PLATE 4.

Before cutting a segment ring make certain that the loaded miter gauge is sliding smoothly but not too loosely in its table groove and then traverse with a steady, uniform, forward pressure. Our experience has shown that operators using the same sawbench set-up produce rings with varying diameters and that minor adjustments and dummy runs are essential to produce perfect assemblies. Very slight lateral pressure or variation in the traverse rhythm can produce an unsatisfactory assembly. Of course some minor faults cancel out and an observant operator soon learns how to cope with the more obvious ones and should not be discouraged by early setbacks. Remember to draw the miter gauge back to the segment stop, to turn over the workstrip, register it with the segment template and fix or hold it firmly against the miter fence before each segment is cut.......and always keep the saw sharp and properly set.

When considerable quantities of segments are wanted and if the ripfence extends from the front to the rear of the table, it is more convenient to employ a stop block form of segment template. This is fixed to the surface of the table with a "C" or "G" clamp and the ripfence moved well clear of the saw or removed completely. This allows the sawn segments to accumulate with small risk of damage from vibratory creep or other hazards when the saw is in motion. Photograph 5 shows this alternative stop block template arrangement.

There are several efficient and fairly expensive types of clamping devices that can be used to assemble rings and discs. We prefer to make ours from 1/2" to 3/4" steel band of the packaging kind which can be picked up for the asking in most timber yards that handle plywood etc. PLATE 5 and photograph 9 show how the band is fitted with cleats and rivets, drawn together by means of a machine screw and square nut to form an effective clamp. The length of the band must be carefully related to the outer circumference of the loosely assembled segmentation. Small segmentations up to say 6" in diameter can be clamped by the familiar hose connecting type of ring which is easily adjusted and moderately priced.

Do not use impact or quick setting adhesive until you have gained experience in assembly routine, taking particular notice of the time required for coating all the segments. Make certain that the loose assembly is flat, circular and correct in pattern before applying adhesive and enough pressure to secure snug joints. When large numbers of components are to be coated for one assembly quickly, it helps to arrange them between slats on scrap board for batch application of adhesive.

RING cylinders have long been used in the pursuit of economy and stability. Examples are stock converted into hollow woodware with modest dimensions such as biscuit barrels, tobacco boxes and drinking vessels. These were first turned in one wood and no serious attempt made to match or oppose the grain patterns in adjacent segments or to create any distinctive surface decoration. In recent times segments have often been comprised of several woods arranged in regular or random sequence, sometimes with checkered features.

After assembly a cylinder is turned true with a recess for its base, and glued in place before fractional change occurs in the overall shape. The final profile is turned with the base attached to a faceplate which allows the rough interior to be tooled smooth and often fitted with a separate container.

Identical flat segment rings can be produced in quantity as transverse sections or ring cylinders if the asssemblies are perfectly matched and clamped up without distortions.

Drafting and computation to ascertain the number and dimensions of cylinder segments is similar to that required for flat ring components. The sawing routine is simple on a sawbench which is provided with a canting table or a tilting arbor saw. The ripping operation of a flat board is reversed for alternate cuts. PLATE 4 explains the sawbench setting with a canting table, selected more for convenience in illustration than for a machine preference.

Ring cylinders down to 1" diameter with a dozen segments can be readily assembled in this form from which scarf rings, needle boxes and napkin rings can be turned, several blanks being crosscut from one assembly.

SECTOR assemblies have a wide decorative field in segmentation because they contain many significant shapes which constitute the main surface of the stock which is seldom lost in the finished turnery. Whole sectors can be sawn in one wood, in a number of species or from built up strips containg a colorful range of carefully proportioned widths. They can be straight lined, curved, or irregular shaped sectors, separated or intersected with thin strips of contrasting veneer and never cease to provide unique polychromatic assemblies.

Straight sectors are an extension of the segment ring principle, produced by a similar sawing procedure applied to a strip wide enough to secure sector sides equal in length to the radius of the major segment chord. Absolute precision in the sawbench set up and operation is needed to deliver sectors which register perfectly with the center point of the assembly. This can be regularly achieved with practice to avoid the expedient of introducing a core to diffuse the closing errors. A central circle sometimes improves the pattern but should not be used to relax craft standards always needed to obtain satisfactory assemblies.

Shaped sectors are usually cut by bandsaw from a tier of solid wood discs in different hues and species held together by a glued paper interleaf or double sided pressure sensitive tape. A full size drawing of the sector arrangement is required which is transferred by carbon paper impression to the surface of the top disc. The sectors are numbered in sequence on the top and side surfaces of the tier and after sawing the layers are separated and rearranged in a recurring color pattern without changing their vertical numerical order. Thus an initial tier of three wood species will produce three disc assemblies in a three colored sector pattern with well matched joints.

The accuracy of sector joints will depend on correct alignment of the saw during operation so it is important to avoid tier heights that overload the machine or feeding conduct that might cause it to deliver sectors with non-vertical sides.

It is possible to produce sectors from templates under jig control but this method is outside our experience and the intended scope of the monograph.

Shaped sector discs are assembled by band clamps and chiefly required for shallow, single tier turnery but they can be introduced into assemblies with solid stock to produce ornamental vases etc. of the types shown in PLATES 31-33.

More complicated patterns can be obtained by reversing the initial pattern in a third assembly as shown in PLATE 22 bearing in mind that the degree of accuracy in tier register must be near perfect to secure an acceptable appearance when components are reduced to very small dimensions. Patterns for these twice sawn assemblies should be checked by means of overlays drafted on transparent material before any sawing takes place.

Shaped sectors are easily marked out by means of a template made in thin, rigid, transparent material which pivots in the center of the pattern to meet appropriate points on its perimeter. A large circular protractor is a great help when fixing these points which can of course be more laboriously determined by dividers.

PLATE 2

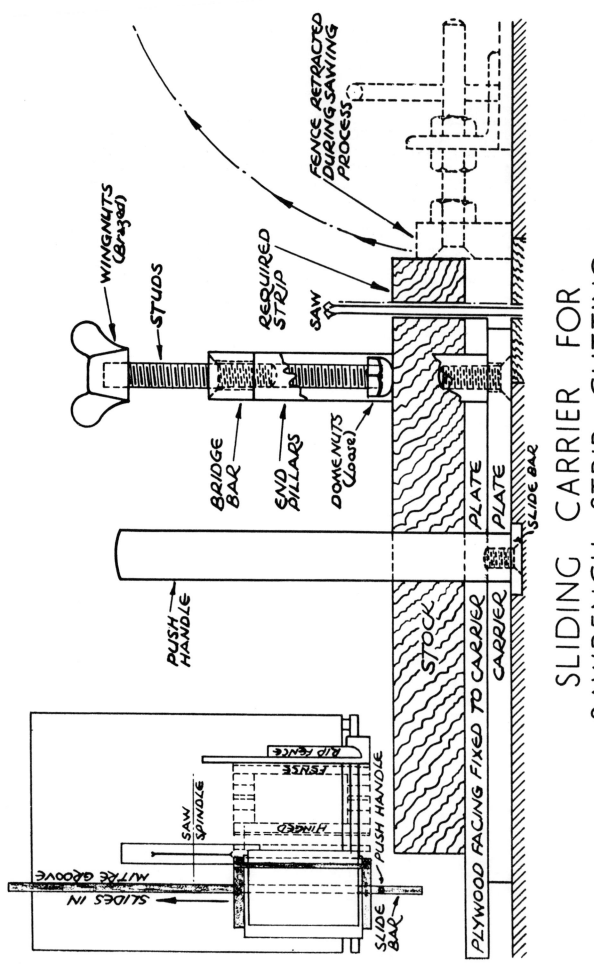

SLIDING CARRIER FOR
SAWBENCH STRIP CUTTING
One eighth & actual size

PLATE 3

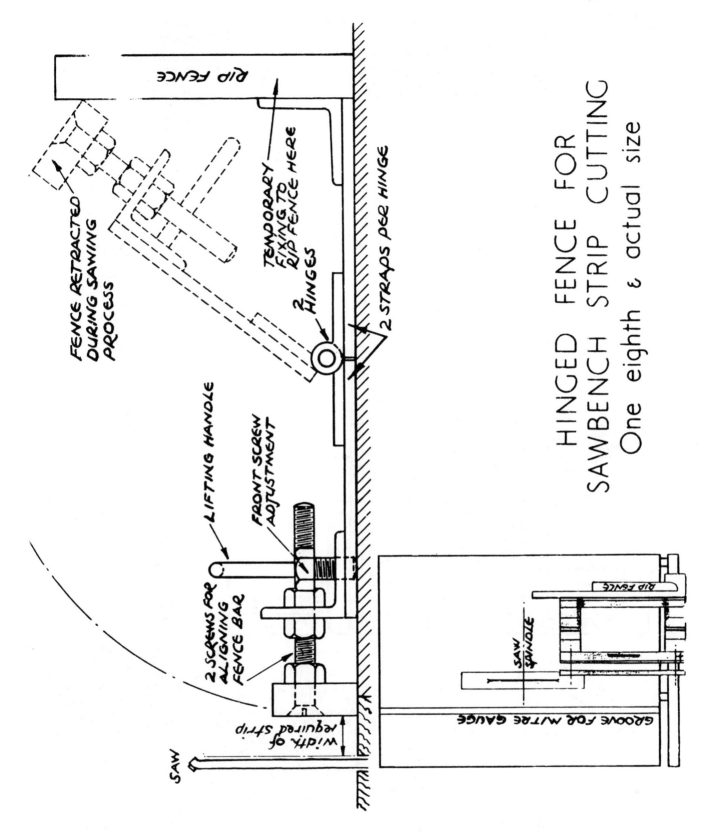

HINGED FENCE FOR
SAWBENCH STRIP CUTTING
One eighth & actual size

RIP FENCE

FENCE RETRACTED DURING SAWING PROCESS

TEMPORARY FIXING TO RIP FENCE HERE

2 HINGES

2 STRAPS PER HINGE

LIFTING HANDLE

FRONT SCREW ADJUSTMENT

2 SCREWS FOR ALIGNING FENCE BAR

Width of required strip

SAW

RIP FENCE

SAW SPINDLE

GROOVE FOR MITRE GAUGE

PLATE 4

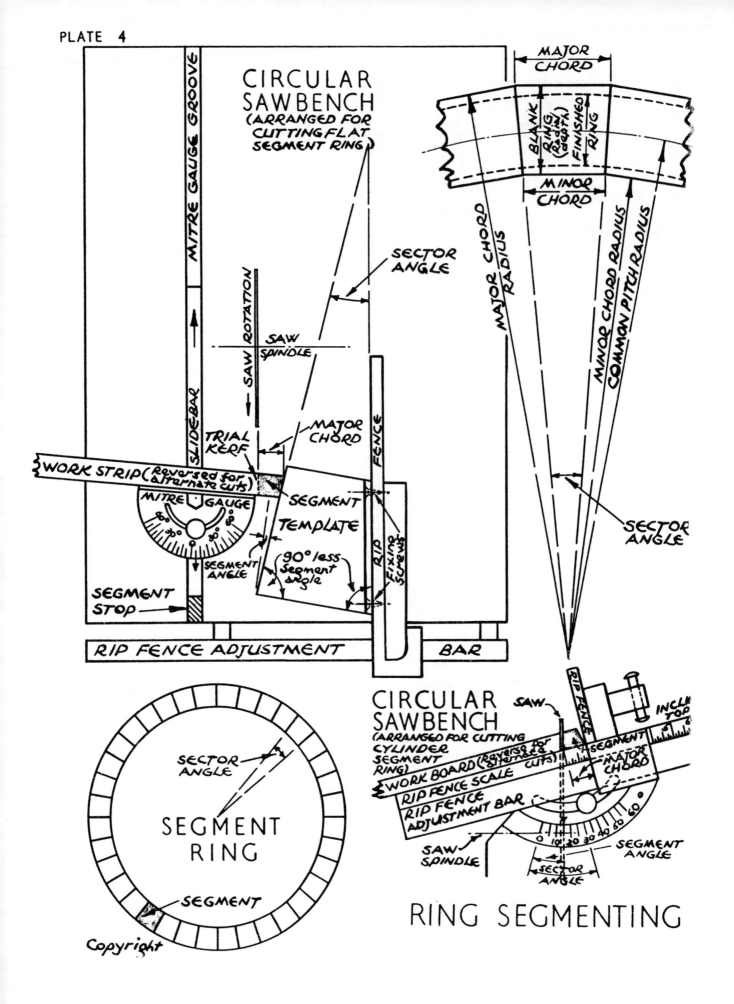

CIRCULAR
SAWBENCH
(ARRANGED FOR
CUTTING FLAT
SEGMENT RING)

MITRE GAUGE GROOVE

SECTOR ANGLE

SAW ROTATION

SAW SPINDLE

SLIDE BAR

TRIAL KERF

MAJOR CHORD

WORK STRIP (Reversed for alternate cuts)

MITRE GAUGE

SEGMENT TEMPLATE

90° less Segment angle

SEGMENT ANGLE

RIP FENCE

Fixing Screws

SEGMENT STOP

RIP FENCE ADJUSTMENT   BAR

MAJOR CHORD

BLANK RING (Radial depth)

FINISHED RING

MINOR CHORD

MAJOR CHORD RADIUS

MINOR CHORD RADIUS

COMMON PITCH RADIUS

SECTOR ANGLE

SECTOR ANGLE

SEGMENT RING

SEGMENT

Copyright

CIRCULAR
SAWBENCH
(ARRANGED FOR CUTTING
CYLINDER
SEGMENT
RING)

SAW

INCLINED TOP

WORK BOARD (Reverse for alternate cuts)

RIP FENCE

SEGMENT

MAJOR CHORD

RIP FENCE SCALE

RIP FENCE
ADJUSTMENT BAR

SAW SPINDLE

0 10 20 30 40 50 60

SECTOR ANGLE

SEGMENT ANGLE

RING SEGMENTING

PLATE 5

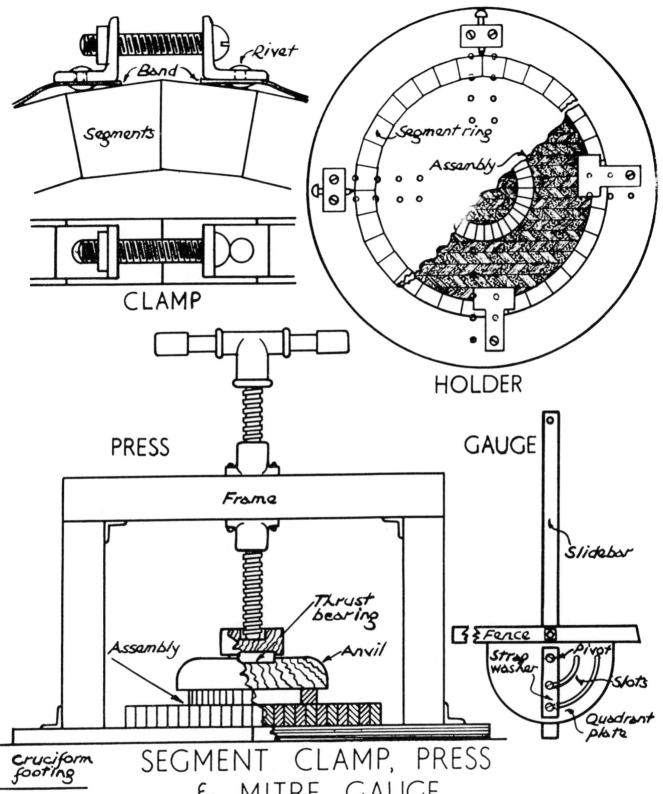

SEGMENT CLAMP, PRESS
& MITRE GAUGE,
DISC TURNING HOLDER
One quarter & actual size

SEGMENT CLAMP, PRESS & MITER GAUGE, DISC & RING TURNING HOLDER.

The accessories illustrated on PLATE 5, and Photographs 5-7 and 9-12 are all of the "Make them yourself" variety and as they are directly related to polychromatic requirements may be considered functionally superior to their nearest proprietory equivalents and will certainly cost less if you have the time and will to make them.

They have no unique or difficult design features, being simple aids for machine sawing, turning and assembly routine connected with the typical projects presented in subsequent plates, photographs and text. Made from stock materials by means of normal workshop tools and facilities, we regard them as basic equipment for polychromatic work which have proved satisfactory over a long period. Variations and alternatives can be easily devised and often have to be improvised to cope with unusual details of certain advanced assemblies.

SEGMENT CLAMP

This was described on Page 29 and because of its simplicity and cheapness we think it best to make a clamp for each diameter of ring or disc assembly required. It would be an improvement to the arrangement shown if the steel band could be welded to the angle cleats but we have not experienced any serious alignment difficulty from the small offset caused by the rivet heads which should be of a flat type, ground or filed flatter when considered helpful on small assemblies. (See photographs 9 and 23.)

PRESS

An old letter press is a readymade form that works well enough for large assemblies when carefully manipulated; but it is a ponderous, insensitive and not very accessible contraption to employ for small circular work. We advise the construction of a more resilient, easily transported type of press, using timber, plywood, a stock press screw fitting and a few woodscrews and carriage bolts.

The press illustrated on PLATE 5 and Photograph 7 has given perfect service for a decade in the U.S.A. using an ordinary wood vise screw and housing in an oak frame fixed to a wooden base with angle iron cleats. The down pressure is distributed by a circular wooden block divided and recessed to house a roller thrust bearing and operates as an anvil plate to cover the diameter of any suitable assembly.

Another press made recently in England is shown on Photograph 21 and this employs a Jorgenson press screw and housing, 9" long by 11/16" diameter, carried by a beech frame composed of a rectangular beam supported by two turned pillars attached to a laminated base 1" thick via through carriage bolts, nuts and washers. Pressure is distributed by means of a swivel foot screwed to a circular steel plate matched approximately to the diameter of the assembly. It can be faced with wood whenever this is considered more friendly to the job in hand.

The bases of both presses are fitted with cruciform footings 2" deep which permits the use of C or G clamps when extra peripheral pressure is required. The

English version has the foot members located diagonally between the pillars which gives maximum access for this purpose. It is also inscribed with circles on the upper surface of the base to assist in centralizing the assembly under the anvil plate. As it weighs only 13 pounds it can be used and stored almost anywhere and its all around visible and manual accessibility with finger sensitive adjustment makes it an ideal form of press for many other workshop jobs.

DISC & RING TURNING HOLDER

This is best turned from a 3/4" block or laminated board screwed to a large faceplate which registers in a shallow recess. Two types of carrier blocks in sets of four are used to secure the larger types of segmented or blocked assemblies to the surface of the holder during turning operations. (Photographs 10, 11, 12.)

To convert the inner and outer chord edges of assemblies into true circles, rectangular hardwood blocks slightly less thick than the segments, are employed. They are attached to the holder by pairs of $\frac{1}{4}$" diameter screws with countersunk heads and nuts via clearance holes that radiate at 1" intervals from its center to cope with a full range of work, the blocks being positioned for inside or outside duty as appropriate. They are also drilled with clearance holes for $\frac{1}{4}$" roundhead screws on a centerline parallel with the holder surface, nuts being inserted in matched recesses at the ends remote from the screw heads. The points of the screws are sharpened so that they penetrate the circular edges of the assembly enough to hold it securely when lateral pressure is applied by a screwdriver, after the work has been centralized by means of circles inscribed on the surface of the holder.

To fix an assembly to the holder after its perimeter has been turned true, tee blocks are used, attached by countersunk head screws and nuts via one of the paired series of holes already described. The tee part of the blocks are felted and may be stepped to suit the profile of the assembly they clip down when this seems worthwhile for greater security on some heavy or advanced project.

All salient edges and corners of blocks are rounded and the heads of fixing screws kept well below wood surfaces and a vigilant routine observed to position the toolrest clear of the blocks and work assembly.

MITER GAUGE

It may seem a cheese paring policy to manufacture this kind of gauge when graduated proprietary types are readily available at moderate cost.Even so, we have found it advantageous and economical to make a range of gauges with permanent angular settings for all segment totals frequently required, say from 6 to 50 in rational numerical steps. This saves much setting up time and waste of material in dummy runs. It also encourages the use of polychromatic features in projects when rings can be quickly cut and assembled to satisfy marginal fancies for this kind of embellishment.

The only critical component is the slidebar which must be carefully matched and fitted to the miter groove in the sawbench. It should be not less than 15" long to ensure that it slides without lateral movement throughout its traverse, failing which it cannot be expected to deliver satisfactory segments.

The miter fence can be of any accurately planed rectangular strip of hardwood fixed to the quadrant plate with its inner end sited as close to the saw as practicable, easily achieved by traversing a projecting surplus with the saw in motion. Purchased gauges usually require a wooden facing strip extension to support work close to the saw.

Laminated board not less than $\frac{1}{2}$" thick is very suitable for the quadrant plate which is provided with two slotted arcs for clamping screws and a hole for the pivot, three adjustment aids that can be fixtures on the slidebar with their upper ends threaded for nuts, or screwed into the bar from above the plate, the important requirement being a common link by metal strip on its surface to lock the gauge when the correct setting is established.

GENERAL NOTE

No useful purpose would be served by providing fully detailed or dimensioned drawings of these four devices because they must be constructed to suit individual lathes and sawbenches, the sizes of the assemblies required and the various materials that are locally available.

SINGLE TIER UNIVERSAL BLOCKING PRESS

Presses for single tier block assemblies can be easily made in a variety of forms related to particular patterns, component dimensions, shapes and the quantity of stock required. PLATE 6 (photographs 13, 14) shows a press with general features that can be utilized to cope with most projects that use shallow assemblies with areas up to 21" square or several smaller ones simultaneously when extra bars are employed .

The press is comprised of a steel baseplate $\frac{1}{4}$" thick X 24" square furnished with steel bars 3/4" high X $\frac{1}{2}$" wide to serve as anchor or pressure bars as appropriate.

The baseplate is drilled and tapped for $\frac{1}{4}$" X 1" roundhead machine screws on $1\frac{1}{2}$" centers to form a grid over its entire surface, commencing 3/4" in from the edges. Anchor bars are drilled vertically with clearance holes to correspond with the grid precisely to permit interchanges. Holes for $\frac{1}{4}$" X 2" roundhead machine screws to operate as drivers for loose pressure bars are drilled and tapped horizontally midway between the anchor screw centers. Alternatively, you may prefer to drill clearance holes with countersinks in the baseplate and drill and tap the anchor bars which saves labor and avoids fouling of threads by the adhesive squeezed out during assembly but it is not as convenient when selecting bar positions for multiple operations.

Pressure bars are best left undrilled but a reduction in the number required may be effected if they are drilled for anchorage and driving, accepting the need to clean out all threaded holes fouled by adhesive. Waxing or greasing all the components before use helps to reduce these minor worries.

Multiple use of presses is a matter of individual need and policy which sometimes calls for the use of make-up bars or a marginal increase in width of outer strips to confine an assembly within the range of the driver screws which should not be excessively long or some deflections will occur. It is good practice to apply pressure to both sides of a wide assembly as this helps to avoid slight distortions in the alignments, particularly so when there are considerable differences in the densities of the wood species and width of strips.

The illustration shows two stages of a chevron pattern assembly and bar arrangements to deal with assemblies in 9", 6" and 3" squares and rectangles 21" X 10" and 5" X 3" in one overall operation. When cleared of intermediate bars this press will accomodate the checkers of a board to carry a standard 4" Staunton pattern chess set or an assembly from which a 21" diameter disc can be extracted.

Screws can be obtained with fixed wing or thumb heads that are easy to adjust but a screwdriver with a matched blade operates comfortably in slotted screw heads which last a long time at a minimum cost.

PLATE 6

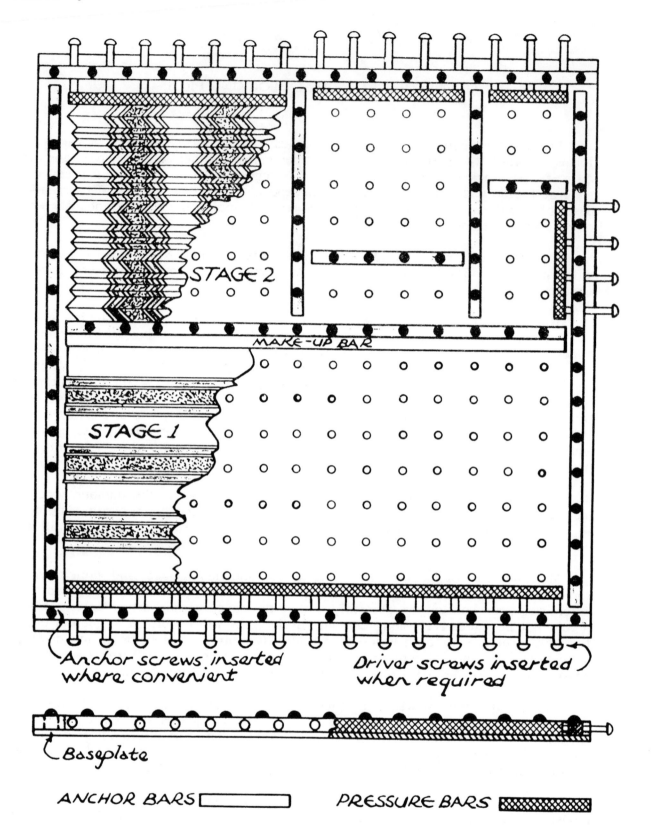

STAGE 2

MAKE-UP BAR

STAGE 1

Anchor screws inserted
where convenient

Driver screws inserted
when required

Baseplate

ANCHOR BARS [   ]   PRESSURE BARS [▨▨▨▨]

UNIVERSAL BLOCKING PRESS
SINGLE TIER
Quarter actual size

PLATE 7

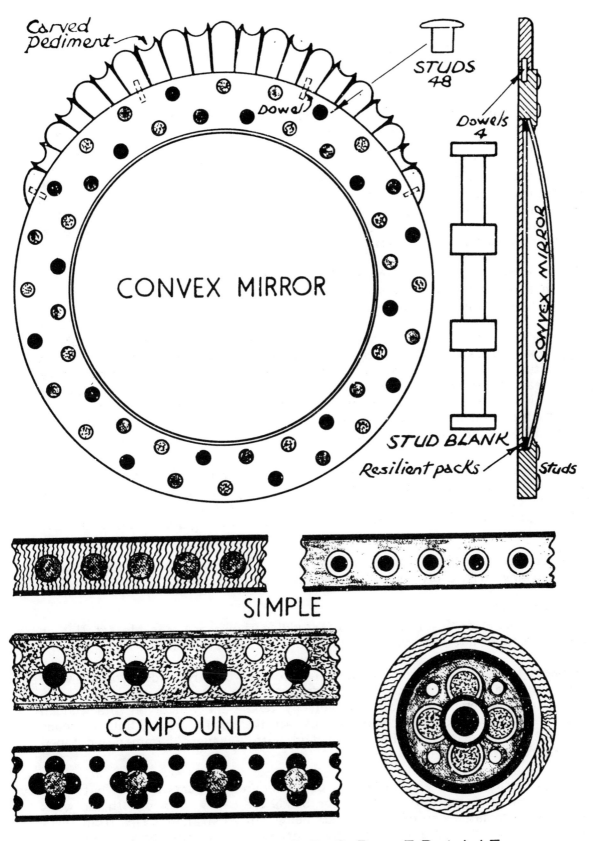

Carved Pediment

STUDS 48

Dowel

Dowels 4

STUD BLANK

Resilient packs

Studs

CONVEX MIRROR

SIMPLE

COMPOUND

STUDDED MIRROR FRAME
AND STUD PATTERNS
One quarter & actual size

STUDDED MIRROR FRAME AND STUD PATTERNS

Large circular frames for pictures or mirrors are seldom turned today, plastic and gesso forms having taken the place of the once popular mahogany and ebonised types. Changes of fashion are frequently due to shortage of suitable materials and in the immediate postwar era it was almost impossible to obtain seasoned timber in England in dimensions for large flat turnery without resorting to segmentation. The frame shown on Plate 7 was therefore turned from a disc of laminated board with a figured oak facing and its outer edge covered with a strip of thick oak veneer. The inner edge was turned with a simple moulding, then painted orange and gilded with leaf.

A pediment was bandsawn from solid oak to match the frame perimeter and glued with a paper interleaf to scrap board to facilitate carving in alternate half rounds and hollows directed towards the center of the mirror.

The face of the frame was decorated with 48 raised studs turned in black, red and ivory colored woods arranged in sequence on two circles with locations offset. Stud blanks were produced from cylinders turned slightly larger than required head diameter, reduced at intervals to stem size, then parted off to correct length. The heads were then completed by gripping the stems in a Jacob's pattern chuck and turning with a chisel, followed by a scraping tool ground to produce the required profile.

The frame was lacquered and polished before the holes for the studs were made by the drill press with its depth gauge in operation. Stud heads were lacquered (3 coats) on a scrap block drilled to receive their stems and when dry were hand polished individually in the lathe chuck, then glued in place without surface residue.

The convex mirror was held snugly in its shaped rabbet by means of a resilient packing strip, a ply backboard and brass finger buttons.

STUD PATTERNS

The four band enclosed patterns of studding shown are suitable for flat or cylindrical surfaces and the large circular one is for a flat central inlay.

Rabbets for enclosing bands on flat surfaces are usually made with the work mounted on a lathe faceplate. The bands are knife cut from thick veneer in segments, using a template or alternatively by taping the veneer on to a wooden faceplate and using a corner chisel to cut out the desired rings, both methods rather wasteful in material. Bands are laid with a veneer hammer and taped down until the glue has set.

On cylinderical surfaces, studding is best executed on parts that do not taper or vary otherwise in profile. Rabbets for bands are easily formed with the work mounted between lathe centers, the bands being cut as straight strips from thick veneer or purchased as plain or patterned strings. They must be held in place with rubber bands or tight cords until the adhesive has set. Some kind of jig should be devised to hold and present the work squarely to the drill press, portable electric drill or hand drill when making holes for studs. Sometimes it is easier - to make up the entire pattern as a flat block and saw this into a veneer for use as a direct inlay when studs are required to finish flush with the surface of the cylinder.

We have only limited experience of compound studding but suggest it is a very suitable form of decoration for owners of ornamental turning lathes to whom we recommend THE ART OF POLYCHROMATIC AND DECORATIVE TURNING by G.A. & B. Audsley published in 1916, a splendidly illustrated volume in terms of the narrow field of polychromatic work it expounds.

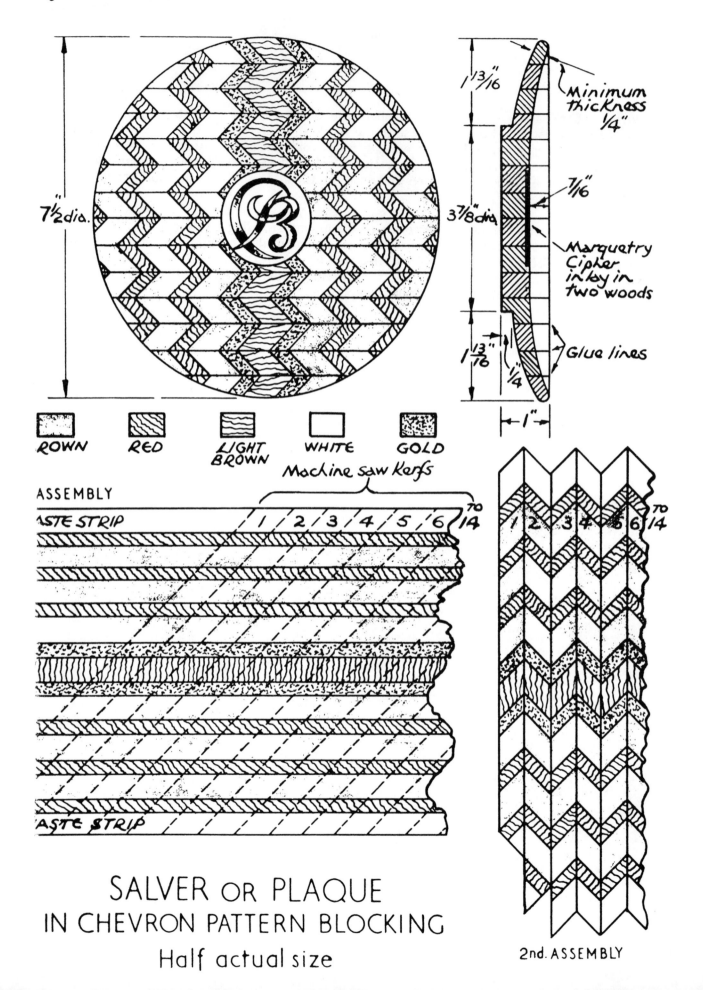

7½" dia.

1 13/16"

3 7/8" dia.

1 13/16"

Minimum thickness ¼"

7/16"

Marquetry Cipher inlay in two woods

Glue lines

¼"

1"

BROWN   RED   LIGHT BROWN   WHITE   GOLD

Machine saw kerfs

ASSEMBLY

PASTE STRIP

1 / 2 / 3 / 4 / 5 / 6 / TO 14

PASTE STRIP

1 2 3 4 5 6 TO 14

2nd. ASSEMBLY

SALVER OR PLAQUE
IN CHEVRON PATTERN BLOCKING
Half actual size

SALVER OR PLAQUE IN CHEVRON PATTERN BLOCKING

Next to the familiar checkered form of flat blocking the chevron pattern is most used and because of the angles at which the opposing rows of components meet more difficult to produce with accurate registration and to avoid considerable waste of material. It is an attractive pattern which can be made arrestive or tastefully interesting, depending on the choice of wood hues, their dispositions and the widths of strips employed.

When only one wood species is used a delicate pattern sheen results to which further interest can be introduced by enclosing the turned disc with a segmented ring.

The example shown on PLATE 8 is a very simple chevron arrangement in which waste side strips are used so that the final assembly is compact on the required chevron perimeter during extraction from the polychromatic blank. This is screwed to a faceplate and the rear of the plaque turned first with a base $\frac{1}{4}$" deep, gripped by the jaws of a self-centering chuck when the front is shaped.

The 2 ply marquetry containing the cypher is made oversize and secured to a blockboard disc with double sided adhesive tape and turned into a circular inlay with a slightly undercut perimeter. After lifting it is carefully fitted into a recess in the plaque fractionally deeper than its 2 ply thickness by gradually opening the recess until a comfortable seating is achieved. This must not be too tight or buckling of the veneers and a bad glue line will occur. When the inlay is secure the surplus depth is removed by a delicate skim with a razor sharp tool and the entire plaque front sanded smooth.

As lathe tools always meet chevron components at opposing angles there is an increased tendency for the wood fibers to tear and the abundance of glue lines quickly blunts cutting edges so remember to sharpen tools more frequently and apply them gently so that snatching and digging in is avoided. If your lathe has a reversing switch it will help to produce a blemish free surface by turning on alternate sides of the work.

When convenient it is good practice to glue all the plain strips for the first assembly of chevron pattern stock in one compressive operation. It is safer as regards registration to glue in stages, starting with pairs, then fours etc. to arrive at the second assembly. Errors due to differing wood strip conduct under compression is less serious in second assembly strips and easier to control.

Photograph 25 shows a more advanced form of Single Tier Chevron Blocking used in the construction of a 16" diameter plate with a planted segmented rim and base. Its square central motif, enclosing borders and strings are of Navajo Indian character set in a background of plain chevron strips, making a total of 840 components in ten wood species.

PLATE 9

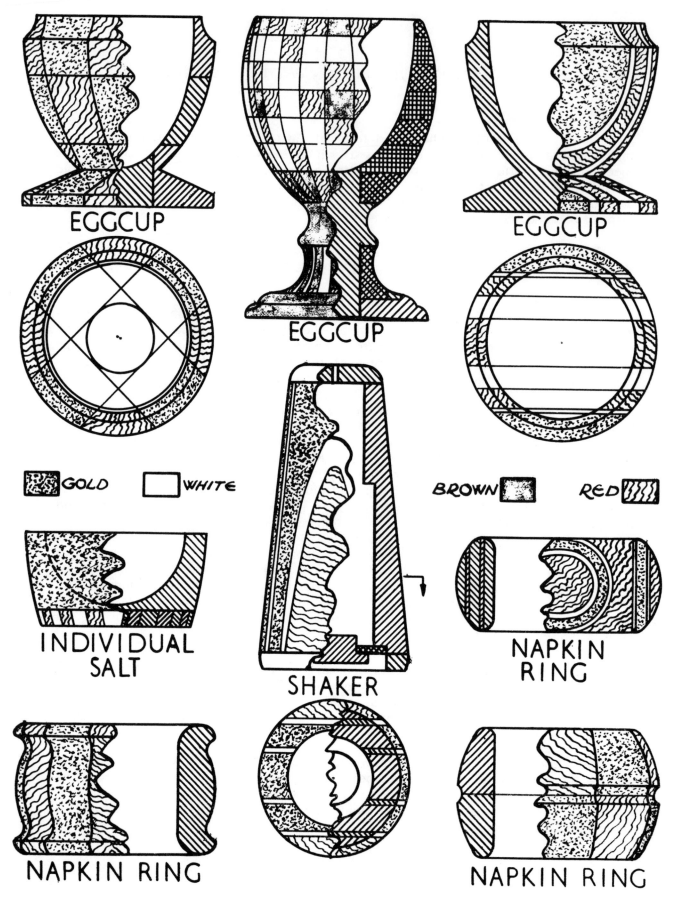

EGGCUP

EGGCUP

EGGCUP

GOLD   WHITE

BROWN   RED

INDIVIDUAL SALT

SHAKER

NAPKIN RING

NAPKIN RING

NAPKIN RING

POLYCHROMATIC TABLEWARE Actual size

POLYCHROMATIC TABLEWARE

No collection of small polychromatic articles is likely to be without examples of tableware some items of which are ideal for using up choice offcuts and reserve assemblies from larger projects or for getting the feel of this fascinating form of wood construction.

With the exception of the large Eggcup, all the articles illustrated in PLATE 9 are of simple basic form and assembly. They require no advanced turning technique or expensive equipment to produce, yet furnish a useful insight into the mechanics of the work and the patterns which emerge from various kinds of sawn wood arrangements.

Standing Salts in elaborate ornamental designs for ceremonial occasions, heirlooms and presentations have been commissioned and produced in a multitude of choice and often precious materials for many centuries. The Worshipful Company of Turners offered medals in 1969 for a Standing Salt to be used at the high table of their dinners, hardwood being the specified material. How many turners are familiar with the small Individual Salt made by early Colonial craftsmen in almost miniature dimensions? We have found this a delightful subject to use up tiny scraps of exotic hardwood in combination with an offcut from a segment ring prepared for a button.

Shakers are one of the favorite projects of American hobby turners who produce them in a wide variety of shapes and wood species, occasionally with elementary polychromatic features. Unless the wood for plain turnery is dense and has a nonporous end grain it is customary and beneficial to cap the Shaker with contrasting wood suitably sawn to avoid exposed end grain on the top surface. Although caps with inset shoulders undoubtedly improve the strength of the glue lines we have not found this refinement necessary in such small articles . . . nor have we discovered the perfect size of hole for the release of the favored condiment.

Napkin rings look well in most polychromatic forms and should be of adequate cross section and avoid thin laminates which run close to their surfaces. The most serviceable type of ring is that which has a solid inner tube to which the outer decorative features are glued. We prefer all our rings to carry a pronounced radius for the admission of the linen and because they are frequently fiddled with, find it seemly to employ shapes which handle smoothly and act as stress relievers.

Sugar Sifters, Pepper Mills, Cheese Boards, Carving Blocks, and Bon-Bon Dishes are other forms of tableware that can be attractively fashioned from polychromatic assemblies.

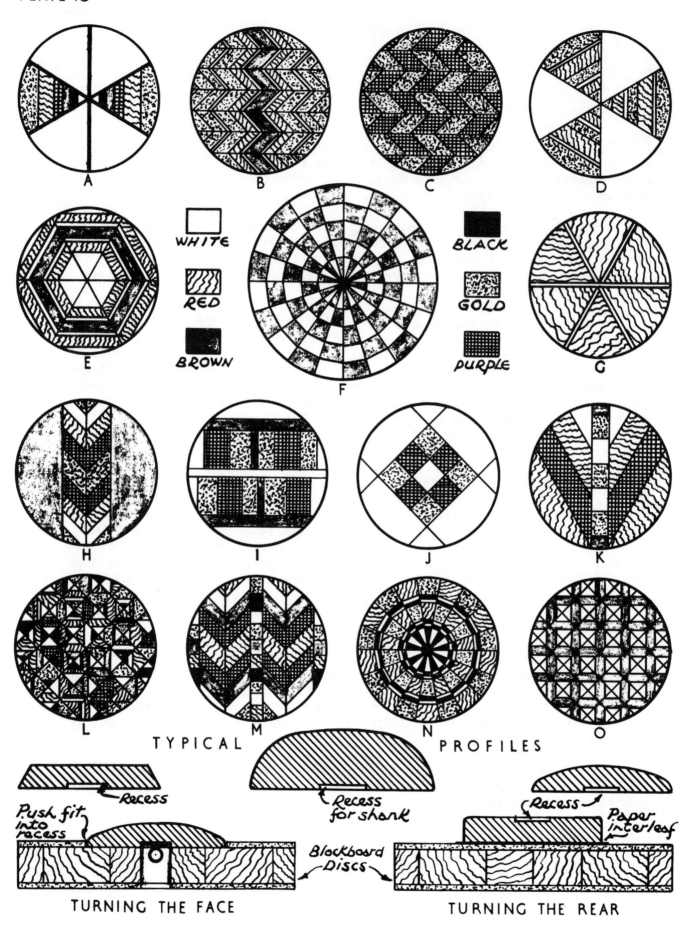

PLATE 10

WHITE

RED

BROWN

BLACK

GOLD

PURPLE

TYPICAL PROFILES

Recess

Recess for shank

Recess

Push fit into recess

Paper interleaf

Blockboard Discs

TURNING THE FACE

TURNING THE REAR

POLYCHROMATIC BUTTONS   Actual size

POLYCHROMATIC BUTTONS

One of the popular hobbies of American ladies is collecting buttons in all sizes, shapes, patterns and materials. They have an enthusiastic Society with branches in many states so it was inevitable that any native exponent of polychromatic wood turnery would get around to making buttons if only to utilize accumulated offcuts from larger projects. (PLATE 10, photograph 40)

No form of small wooden article offers wider scope for decorative assemblies in geometric or abstract patterns which can also be employed in brooches, medallions, tie bolos, small mats and inlays for larger turned surfaces.

The best and worst examples of polychromatic assembly can be utilized for button blanks, the near perfect ones for designs like B, C, E, F, N and O in which geometric precision is essential for connoisseur acceptance, less so with A, D, G, J and M which are more open patterns and much less so for H, I, K and L that are obviously suitable for random offcuts. All these buttons shown on PLATE 10 can be made in single tier blocking or flat ring and straight sector segmenting from a range of six woods with distinct color contrasts that will provide attractive variety in the finished articles.

As polychromatic buttons are seldom used for purposes other than collection display, they are made larger than most functional types. $1\frac{1}{4}$" diameter X $\frac{1}{4}$" thick are a suitable size. They are turned from blanks assembled from strips 1/32" to $\frac{1}{2}$" thick (generally thinner than $\frac{1}{4}$") and segments with a radius of 3/4" are cut from multiple or plain strips 1" wide.

Buttons made in single tier blocking are turned from square or octagonal assemblies and segmented ones from oversize circles, all tape mounted and accurately centered on turned wood discs attached to faceplates or more conveniently held by the jaws of a self-centering chuck. The back of a button is turned first with a recess for its shank, glued in place before the reversal for face turning. This is executed in a second wood disc by means of a press fit into a shallow recess with a central clearance hole for the shank. Epoxy resin adhesive is ideal for shank fixing.

Collectors prefer small shanks which seat snugly on their display boards and it is possible to purchase jewellery fittings which meet this requirement. A more robust alternative that also serves a sartorial need is by using small metal buttons of the blazer type about $\frac{1}{2}$" in diameter. By sinking a recess that corresponds with the curved face of the button, a little lower than the rear surface of the blank, it is easy to employ the entire button as a shank which then has a very substantial seating. An interesting sidelight is that shanks can no longer be purchased in Birmingham where they were invented except by large special order because it is now cheaper to buy them from abroad.

When assemblies are made specifically for buttons it is economical to select a depth that can be sawn to supply at least two sets of blanks. Excessive depth or over pressure during assembly may lead to vertical misalignments of components. When these are detected try to strike a mean location when centering a blank for turning. It is essential for the production of satisfactory blanks that the sawing and assembly routine is as near perfect as possible. Only sharp saws and precise miter gauge settings can supply suitable components.

Button profiles are kept simple as their appearance depends chiefly upon the pattern which can be impaired by messy turnery details. All surfaces are lacquered by brush and polished on the lathe by methods we have described for other projects.

We have not produced any link types of button similar to those used on duffle coats. These could be easily turned from multi-tiered spindle blocking with a strong central core, rather like the assemblies of geometric shapes found in Tunbridge stickware.

Another form of decorative button could be made by inlays of compound studding in a matrix of contrasting plain wood.

ORNAMENT IN SPINDLE BLOCKING

Some of our early polychromatic assemblies were made for Table Lamp Standards, the arrangement in PLATE 11 being equally suitable for lamps or ornaments. It can also be scaled down by one third within the safe working limits of the design when its height is considered in excess of requirement as it was originally produced for American homes and sized accordingly.

Some of its small components have been omitted to simplify illustration and the wood colors limited to six whereas we frequently used a dozen to provide extra interest for wood lovers. Our main purpose in presenting this design was to give some indication of the pattern forms and color distribution that emerges from a shrewd arrangement of rectangular blocks and strips when turned into a simple conventional shape.

If you decide to develop an original polychromatic project it will be possible to determine some of its main pattern features from a scale drawing of cross sections and elevations but unless your projection skill is better than ours it will be easier and quicker to make up a trial assembly. This should be turned slowly into the desired profile, taking great care not to reduce diameters beyond safe margins when approaching longitudinal joint lines, particularly so when components are known to be of thin cross sections.

Our example consists of three major groupings of components assembled around a common 1 3/8" square core. This was given a central bore of 5/16" diameter and end plugged for turning support, or halved and stop grooved when used as a conduit for lamp wiring. A separate square base of solid wood was sometimes given a checkered margin by rabbeting its upper surface to receive the strips and drilled to take the dowel end of the turned column.

All strips and blocks were produced on the sawbench by the methods and equipment already described, making all cuts of similar dimensions from single settings of the hinged fence, the best insurance against bad registrations in assemblies and tedious surface adjustments.

We have purposely omitted most of the secondary joint lines on the drawing because the manner in which minor assemblies are made will depend on the clamping equipment, lengths of wood and time available, also personal choice of ganging stages. Our general procedure was to start with the center group by making up a pair of minor opposite sides, followed by their corresponding and abutting minor assemblies for top and bottom groups. This provided a stage with maximum level surfaces on two sides to which the remaining full width minor assemblies were added in any convenient combinations. The center group then required the addition of its outside locking components.

Turning was a straight forward job and after sanding and brush lacquering, all polishing and burnishing was completed with the lathe in motion, except the sides of the square base.

PLATE 11

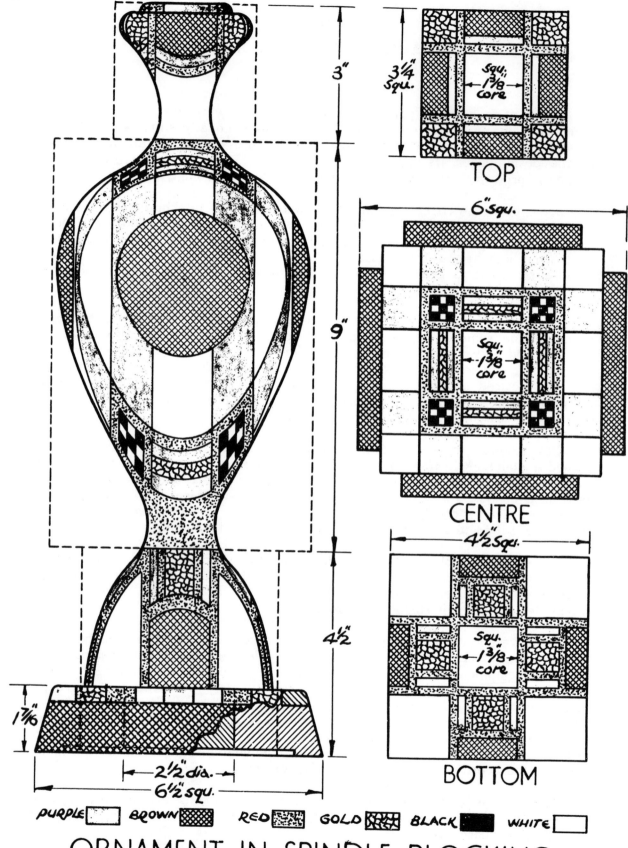

3"

9"

4½"

3¼"
squ.

squ.
1⅜
core

TOP

6"squ.

squ.
1⅜
core

CENTRE

4½"squ.

squ.
1⅜
core

BOTTOM

1⁷⁄₁₆"

2½"dia.

6½"squ.

PURPLE   BROWN   RED   GOLD   BLACK   WHITE

ORNAMENT IN SPINDLE BLOCKING
Half actual size

SEGMENTED TRINKET BOWL & POSY & CANDLE HOLDER
Plate 12

Of the many small domestic articles turned on a faceplate or some form of chuck, perhaps the most popular and in consequence most difficult to produce in an attractive original design, is the nut or trinket bowl.

Bowls in simple polychromatic checkered patterns of common hardwoods having strong color contrasts are often made commercially, stock for which can be sometimes purchased for hobby requirements. But the discerning specialist turn er is not likely to enthuse over such "Do it Yourself" offers which present little challenge to expertise and seldom satisfy aesthetic requirements.

Segment rings assembled in selected combinations of elegant hardwoods can be introduced as decorative bands into turnery for a host of familiar articles   to provide unique features without detriment to utility, strength or general acceptablility.

The Trinket Bowl illustrated is composed of five rings, four segmented and one solid with a base plug and a small interior segmented inlay. The turning blank was formed by gluing the segment rings together in tier, followed by a solid disc for the rim. This allowed the blank to be screwed to a faceplate so that the cavity for the base plug could be turned and with a slight drift on the side to ensure a tight glue fit. The plug was turned on a second faceplate and in a depth which kept the screw holes clear of the bowl bottom when released and glued in place to complete the blank.

It was then possible to turn the external profile of the bowl on the first faceplate after which the work was released and returned to the second faceplate for hollowing out and forming a recess for the central inlay. This was then glued down, turned level and the entire job sanded, oiled, lacquered and polished on the lathe. Instead of parting off the bowl whilst held on the faceplate by the surplus wood of the plug we preferred to remount it rim down on to a faceplate lined with waste board which carried four shaped, felted clips that held the work securely without marking the polish while the surplus wood was turned off and a recess cut to receive a table felt.

The Posy and Candle Holder was produced by a different routine. First a disc $\frac{1}{4}$" in excess of the final depth of the project was turned true on its edge and exposed face. Then a channel cut slightly smaller than the cross section and diameter of the segment ring to be fitted. The disc was then parted in the center of the channel after a matching line had been marked on the edge. Although the polychromatic ring would separate the top and bottom tiers of solid wood it was considered desirable to maintain the natural pattern of the grain.

The segment ring was mounted on a second faceplate and its internal edge and exposed face turned to match the shoulder formed by the half channel in that part of the solid disc left on the first faceplate. The ring was removed from its faceplate and glued in place under slight pressure in a bench vise.

PLATE 12

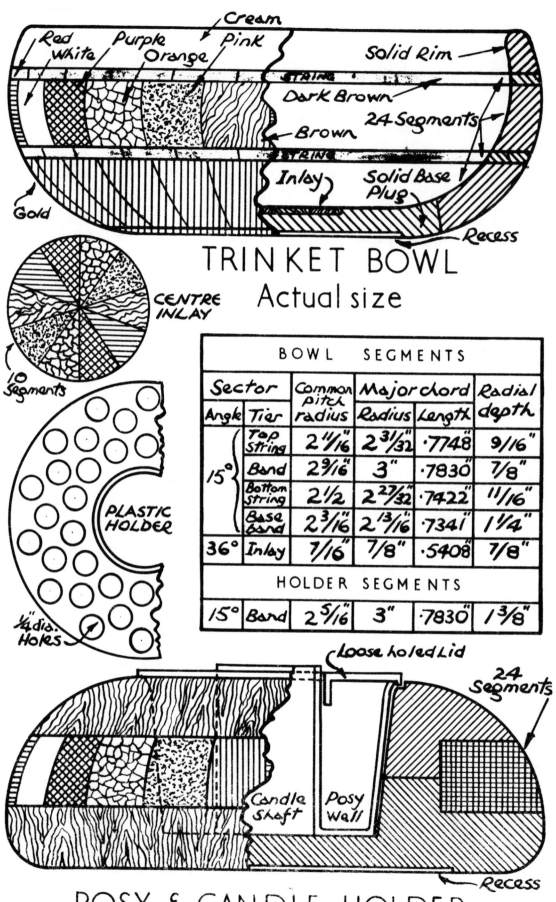

Red · White · Purple · Orange · Cream · Pink · Solid Rim

STRING

Dark Brown

24 Segments

Brown

STRING

Inlay · Solid Base Plug

Gold

Recess

TRINKET BOWL
Actual size

CENTRE INLAY

10 Segments

PLASTIC HOLDER

¼ dia. Holes

BOWL SEGMENTS					
Sector		Common pitch radius	Major chord		Radial depth
Angle	Tier		Radius	Length	
15°	Top String	2¹¹/₁₆″	2³¹/₃₂″	·7748″	9/16″
	Band	2⁹/₁₆″	3″	·7830″	7/8″
	Bottom String	2½	2²⁷/₃₂″	·7422″	11/16″
	Base band	2³/₁₆″	2¹³/₁₆″	·7341″	1¼″
36°	Inlay	7/16″	7/8″	·5408″	7/8″
HOLDER SEGMENTS					
15°	Band	2⁵/₁₆″	3″	·7830″	1³/₈″

Loose holed Lid

24 Segments

Candle Shaft · Posy Wall

Recess

POSY & CANDLE HOLDER
Actual size

The other part of the solid disc was then mounted on the second faceplate and its shoulder turned to match the cavity left in the segment ring part of the first stage of the assembly making certain that the meeting surfaces of the solid discs showed a hairline joint when glued to complete the blank.

As the functional appearance of the project did not expose the cavity for the posy holder, no blemishes from faceplate screw holes had to be avoided and it was a simple routine to turn the external profile, hollow out to receive the plastic holder, then sand, lacquer and polish all the appropriate surfaces with the piece remaining on the original faceplate. . . one of the easiest polychromatic exercises we have devised and also one of the most satisfying when bedecked with a seasonal floral garland around a quality candle.

A note of timely warning now in respect to all projects that incorporate segment rings. The larger the size of the ring and the greater the number used in a job, the more important it is to ensure that all meeting surfaces are level and tier lines parallel or disturbing surface blemishes and undesirable registers will occur.

PLATE 13

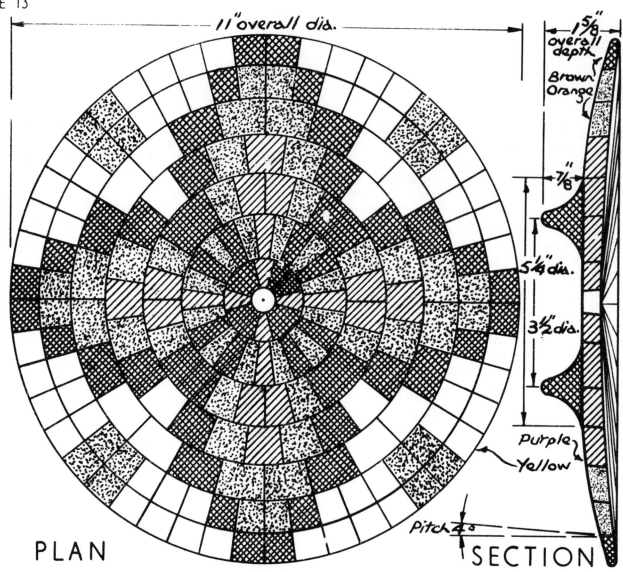

11" overall dia.

1 5/8" overall depth

Brown Orange

7/8"

5 1/4" dia.

3 1/2" dia.

Purple Yellow

Pitch 2.5

PLAN   SECTION

RINGS						SEGMENTS					
SEQUENCE	COMPONENTS					Sector angle	Common pitch radius	Major chord		Radial depth	Common joint radius
	TOTAL	Yellow	Orange	Brown	Purple			Radius	Length		
1 Outer	48	32	8	8	-	7½	5 3/16	5 13/16	.7603	5/8	4 7/8
2	48	24	16	8	-	7½	4 17/32	5 5/32	.6744	11/16	4 3/16
3	24	8	8	8	-	15	3 13/16	4 7/16	1.1582	3/4	3 7/16
4	24	4	8	8	4	15	3 1/32	3 21/32	.9543	13/16	2 5/8
5	24	-	8	8	8	15	2 3/16	2 13/16	.7341	7/8	1 3/4
6	24	4	8	8	4	15	1 9/32	1 29/32	.4975	15/16	13/16
7 Inner	12	-	-	8	4	30	1/2	1 1/8	.5823	5/8	3/16
Centre	circle	1	-	-	-	360	-	-	-	3/16	
TOTALS	205	73	56	56	20	DIMENSIONS EXPRESSED IN INCHES					
LENGTHS EXPRESSED IN FEET		6.5	4.5	4.5	1.5	× 1¼"× 1" } PLANED STOCK (Finish sizes)					
		ATTACHED BASE			.5	× 6" × 1"					

SEGMENTED PLATE
Half actual size

SEGMENTED PLATE

Plate 13

Before commencing work on a fully segmented plate it should be appreciated that this form of construction is an advanced exercise in precision sawing, turning and glued assembly. It can also be regarded as a complicated method for producing a domestic article with simple outlines, liable to prove wasteful in material unless a full scale detail drawing is prepared beforehand supported by an accurate cutting chart and preferably some computations in respect to the components.

We have illustrated a plate of modest dimensions suitable for turning on a center lathe with a 6" radial swing ideally, though not essentially, provided with a compound sliderest and tool holder. Adequate margins for the various machine and tool operations have been allowed for in the component cutting chart but we would stress the advantages of making several plates together since this offers some latitude for interchange of segment rings if minor inaccuracies occur in the turning process.

Use as many colors and species of wood as you fancy; we found four enough for the pattern presented because of limitations in black and white illustration. Our example was executed in well contrasted hues provided by Maple, Padauk, Walnut and Purpleheart represented as yellow, red, brown and purple on the drawing.

The seven segment rings involved were prepared by the methods described in our main article, using a wood section $1\frac{1}{4}$" wide X 1" thick and pitch circles which secured maximum waste margins for major and minor segment chords, the minimum diametrical tolerance being above 1/8".

We tried both rotations for the concentric assembly of segment rings; from the center plug outwards and from the perimeter inwards. With care, both proved satisfactory but we preferred the latter because it offered a longer perimeter for attaching the first ring to the wood clad faceplate by buttons or other preferred device.

The meeting edges of all turned segment rings were given a pitch of 4 degrees by means of a cutter held in the toolpost of the compound sliderest. Having completed the inside edge of one ring, the outside edge of the next ring was turned slightly oversize on a separate faceplate and then gradually fitted by trial and error until it made continuous edge contact with its counterpart facilitated by the pitching which left only trivial surface unevenness at the joint. It was considered prudent if not imperative to apply the adhesive immediately after the fitting of each ring to obviate fractional change in diameter which might occur from delayed assembly. We used a gap filling glue as a precaution against hairline interstices.

The plate components were assembled and one surface was turned to receive the base stock. This was turned a little oversize with its rim fractionally proud of its center to ensure good seating when glued in place. This completed the preliminary and most difficult part of the project.

Of several satisfactory ways in which the plate could then be continued the method adopted was to screw a scrapwood disc to the base stock, insuring this fixture is clear of the final profile. It is then attached to a standard metal faceplate. Care must be taken to check the centricity of the segment rings when the entire assembly is mounted on the lathe.

The top surface of the plate was then turned concave, its perimeter rounded and its underside shaped to the point where it met the rough edge of the planted base. All sanding, lacquering and burnishing of these surfaces was completed before removal from the faceplate.

The work was now reversed and attached to a larger disc holder by buttons and when perfectly centered, the middle of the base turned to waste, thus exposing the segmented pattern. The remaining ring was then turned to a smooth profile and finished as in the frontal procedure, leaving the completed plate free from screw holes, bruises, eccentricity, or sub-standard polishing. The polychromatic purist may prefer to use a segmented ring for the solid type of base we prefer and recommend.

Photograph 26 shows the finished appearance of this plate, not seen to best advantage in monochrome as the hues appear closely related whereas they are well separated in a colored picture.

SEGMENTED PAPERWEIGHT
Plate 14

The paperweight lends itself to a wide variety of shapes and patterns without need to apply hard and fast rules in design or order of component assembly. In fact our first example was evolved from oddments and segments left over from other jobs which, when assembled as an experiment, gave such a pleasing result that we decided to make it a planned project with the addition of a metal core to increase its overall weight. This was cast from scrap lead in a mold formed by drilling a hole part way through a block of scraggy oak.

The article was comprised of two main parts, a knob and the body. The knob was turned in a dense hardwood, inset on top with a small segmented polychromatic disc and provided below with a dowelled stem to fit into the body of the paperweight. This was built up from a number of segment rings of differing patterns, hues and woods around a central hardwood dowel so disposed as to present an attractive external surface pattern above a solid wooden base.

Before assembly, the rings were levelled on both surfaces and reduced to the desired thickness on the lathe, using a self centering 3 jaw chuck and a tool applied from the machine sliderest. A hand turning tool applied from the tool rest would have served equally well. A clearance hole for the insertion of the dowel was made by means of a twist drill advanced by the tailstock handwheel. The rings were glued together in pairs in accordance with the Component Chart, threaded on to a spare piece of dowel, and removed as soon as initial adhesion had been obtained. These glued pairs were then assembled on the final dowel and subjected to mild pressure in a vise after vertical alignment and the addition of the solid base. Minor faults in segment register were expected but when sensibly distributed were not detrimental to the overall appearance of the article since we sought a mosaic effect rather than one of geometric exactitude.

The rough knob and body assemblies were glued together by means of the dowelled stem and it was then possible to grip the knob end in the chuck and drill out the cavity for the lead core from the tailstock end. A plug was turned in scrap wood to give a nice twist fit in this cavity and the work was thus held and supported by the chuck while the profile of the paperweight was turned by hand tools and sanded to a smooth surface. It was considered safer, if not essential, to adopt the precaution of supporting the knob with the tailstock during the roughing out process until the tool rest was turned at right angles to the lathe spindle for the final cuts to the top surface of the knob.

As we polished this kind of article on the lathe, the plug was left in the cavity and used to handle the work while successive coats of clear lacquer were brushed on until a suitable depth was built up and hardened off to permit of cutting down, polishing and burnishing to the required glaze. Then the plug was removed and the lead weight glued in place, covered by a previously turned wooden plug in turn concealed by a disc of thick felt. (Photograph 41).

PLATE 14

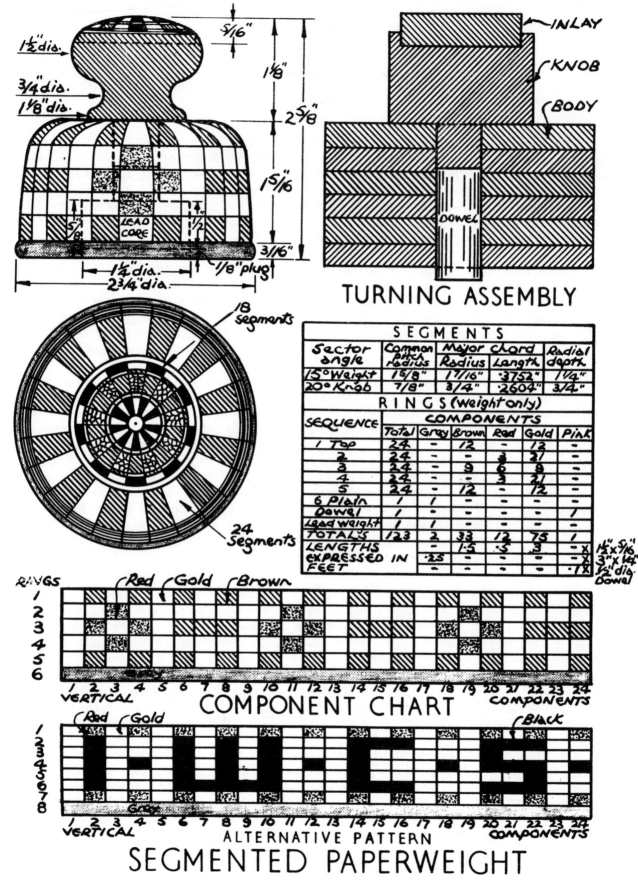

TURNING ASSEMBLY — INLAY, KNOB, BODY, DOWEL, LEAD CORE

18 segments / 24 Segments

SEGMENTS				
Sector angle	Common pitch radius	Major chord Radius	Major chord Length	Radial depth
15° Weight	1⅝"	1 7/16"	·3752"	1¼"
20° Knob	7/8"	3/4"	·2604"	3/4"

RINGS (weight only)						
SEQUENCE	COMPONENTS					
	Total	Gray	Brown	Red	Gold	Pink
1 Top	24	-	12	-	12	-
2	24	-	-	3	21	-
3	24	-	9	6	9	-
4	24	-	-	3	21	-
5	24	-	12	-	12	-
6 Plain	1	1	-	-	-	-
Dowel	1	-	-	-	-	1
Lead weight	1	1	-	-	-	-
TOTALS	123	2	33	12	75	1
LENGTHS EXPRESSED IN FEET		1·5	·5	3	-	-
	·25	-	-	-	-	·1

1½" × 5/16"
3" × 1¼"
½" dia. Dowel

RINGS 1 2 3 4 5 6 — Red, Gold, Brown

COMPONENT CHART
VERTICAL 1 2 3 4 5 6 7 8 9 10 11 12 13 14 15 16 17 18 19 20 21 22 23 24 COMPONENTS

Red, Gold, Black

ALTERNATIVE PATTERN
VERTICAL 1 2 3 4 5 6 7 8 9 10 11 12 13 14 15 16 17 18 19 20 21 22 23 24 COMPONENTS

SEGMENTED PAPERWEIGHT
Actual size

SEGMENTED TABLE LIGHTER
Plates 15 & 16

This Smoker's accessory was designed to accommodate lighter mechanisms known to be available in several countries at moderate cost. We evolved a shape that was comfortably held and operated by one hand and also stable in a free standing table position. From this we prepared a rectangular chart of the polychromatic components at full scale, approximating to the surface area of the proposed cylinder. The chart contained fifteen horizontal bands crossed by twenty four vertical columns representing all the components in outline. A decorative pattern was then marked out in a thrice repeated motif which employed four wood color species, explained by the accompanying illustration. PLATE 16.

The variation between maximum and minimum diameters of the cylinder was only 5/8" so we considered these could be conveniently extracted from rings $2\frac{1}{4}$" diameter each having twenty-four segments with a segment angle of $7\frac{1}{2}°$ degrees, a major chord of 0.2936" and a radial depth of 1" including a minimum tolerance of 1/16".

The eleven segmented rings were of equal thickness in five different patterns, one single, three paired and one quadruplicated. Rings of repeated patterns were made from double thickness stock, halved by saw after the glue assembly, a method which helped to regulate marginal errors invertical alignment of exposed segments during the various stages of the cylinder assembly. The plain rings were made to maximum cylinder diameter. All rings were scribed on flat strips and produced by saw and disc sander to a maximum cylinder diameter. All rings were levelled and thicknessed on the lathe by means of a three jaw self centering chuck. A cutting tool was applied from the compound sliderest. The ring was reversed after the first surface was made true. This work can be executed satisfactorily by hand turning or other workshop techniques.

In the interests of accuracy it was considered expedient to build up the cylinder in easy stages so Ring numbers 2 & 3, 5 & 6, 7, 8 & 9, 10 & 11, 13 & 14 were glued together as pairs and one trio, then returned to the lathe chuck for central drilling with a 3/8" clear hole, using a twist drill in another chuck advanced by the tailstock and handwheel. The plain discs were similarly drilled except No. 15, the bottom one, which was bored only part way to receive the glued end of a piece of 3/8" diameter dowel about 4" long. The final assembly was made by threading the glued rings on to this dowel, being careful to observe the pattern on the chart and obtain the best possible vertical alignment of segments before subjecting the column to mild compression by vise or other simple clamping device. The dowel core is not essential but it does help to simplify a tricky assembly job and does improve the mechanical strength of the cylinder.

The ends of the cylinder were then accurately centered and the polychromatic stock turned true with the driving center engaged in the end to be recessed for the cup of the lighter mechanism. The other end was turned slightly concave to ensure a good table seating, then reversed and the self centering chuck used to hold the work lightly until it was aligned by the tailstock center registered

PLATE 15

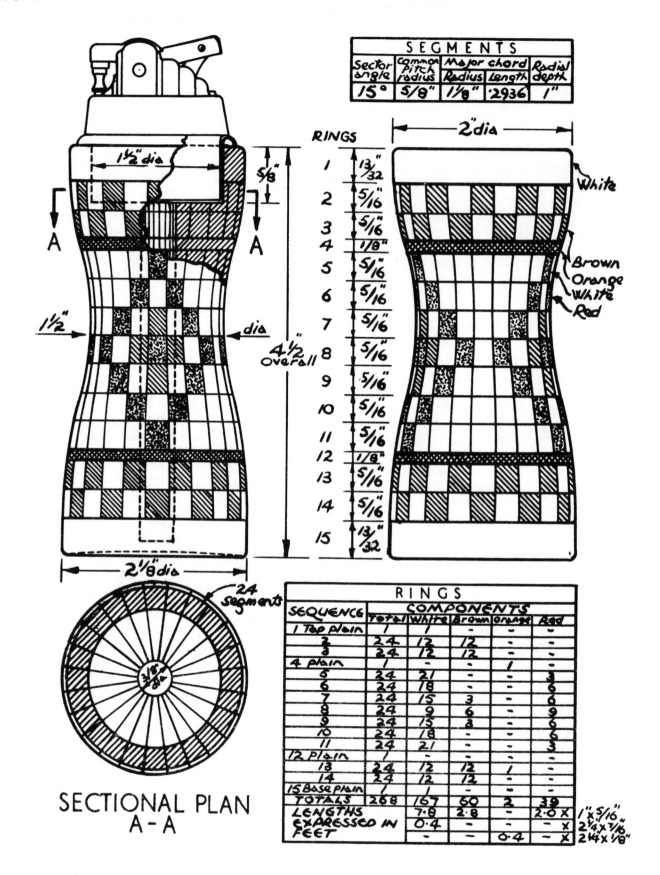

SEGMENTS

Sector angle	Common pitch radius	Major chord Radius	Length	Radial depth
15°	5/8"	1⅛"	·2936	1"

RINGS

1	13/32"
2	5/16"
3	5/16"
4	1/8"
5	5/16"
6	5/16"
7	5/16"
8	5/16"
9	5/16"
10	5/16"
11	5/16"
12	1/8"
13	5/16"
14	5/16"
15	13/32"

4½" Overall

2" dia

White
Brown
Orange
White
Red

1⅛"dia

5/8

1½" dia

2⅛" dia

24 segments

3/8" dia

SECTIONAL PLAN A-A

RINGS

SEQUENCE	COMPONENTS				
	Total	White	Brown	Orange	Red
1 Top plain	1	-	-	-	-
2	24	12	12	-	-
3	24	12	12	-	-
4 plain	1	-	-	1	-
5	24	21	-	-	3
6	24	18	-	-	6
7	24	15	3	-	6
8	24	9	6	-	9
9	24	15	3	-	6
10	24	18	-	-	6
11	24	21	-	-	3
12 plain	1	-	-	-	-
13	24	12	12	1	-
14	24	12	12	-	-
15 Base plain	1	-	-	-	-
TOTALS	268	167	60	2	39
LENGTHS		7·8	2·8	-	2·0 X	1" x 5/16"
EXPRESSED IN		0·4	-	-	- X	2¼ x ⅞"
FEET		-	-	0·4	- X	2¼ x ⅛"

SEGMENTED TABLE LIGHTER
Actual size

PLATE 16

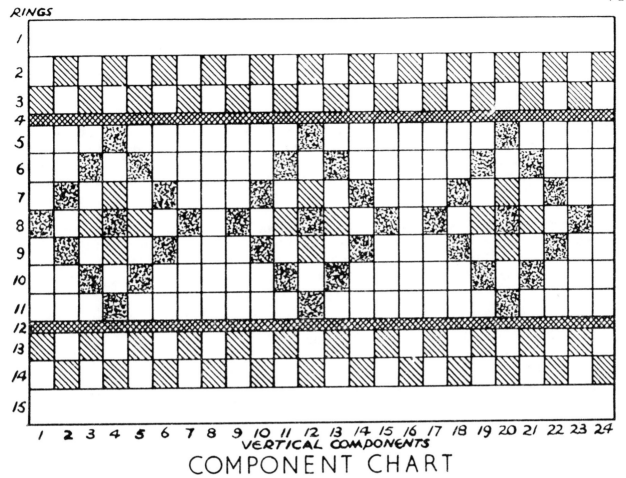

RINGS

VERTICAL COMPONENTS

COMPONENT CHART

☐ WHITE

▨ RED

▧ BROWN

▨ ORANGE

RECESSED FOR LIGHTER CUP

RECESSED FOR LIGHTER CUP

24 Segments

SEGMENTED TABLE LIGHTERS
Actual size

in the original driving center hole. The cup recess was made with a drill advanced by tailstock and handwheel with the lathe in motion Then the cup was fixed in place with a strong resin adhesive and a plug turned in hardwood to make a snug but not force fit in the cup. It was then a simple operation to hand turn the cylinder to its final profile with the assurance it was revolving on centers-accurately related to the segmentation in both planes.

After sanding, the cylinder was given successive brush coats of hard, transparent, synthetic lacquer, cut back between applications with "Wet & Dry" abrasive paper until a surface free from pits and curtains was obtained. This was further improved with levelling paste and finished with burnishing liquid, all processes performed with the lathe in motion.

A felt disc was glued to the bottom surface of the cylinder to obscure the small center hole and serve as a scratch guard.

Two other table lighter shapes which incorporate less complicated polychromatic segmentations with twenty-four segments, are illustrated on PLATE 16. These require both hands for lighter operation.

SEGMENTED GOBLET
Plate 17

This was an experimental project to ascertain how a small turned assembly of segmented rings supported by a slender column would behave when reduced to a bowl shape with thin walls in which the components were not interlocked and survival depended upon the quality of the joints and glue strength in the horizontal and vertical planes. (PLATE 17, photograph 24).

Woods of similar density, known to possess good adhesion qualities were assembled with a strong resin glue left to cure for over a week before considered safe enough for turning. None of the joints opened then or show signs of so doing after several years in an ordinary domestic temperature.

Instead of a uniform geometrical pattern for the principal decorative feature the segments were arranged to present the initials I.W.C.S. in a white wood that contrasted with its background perhaps a mistake as this also accentuated   the small differences of component register in the external surface of the finished turnery. These normally help to soften the stereotyped character of a formal pattern but can be irritating when a motif has to convey a specific meaning.

The goblet is comprised of one major polychromatic assembly linked by a solid stem to a base inlaid with a multi-patterned ring extracted from a segmented button blank. These often prove useful for adding restrained embellishment to an otherwise plain turnery.

The bowl block was turned in a three jaw self-centering chuck and its rough central cavity bored out to a diameter of 3/4" for a depth of 3/4" into which a plug was glued to form the bottom of the interior, leaving part of the hole for later admission of the stem cylinder. The block was then reversed in the chuck, carefully hollowed out and this interior surface sanded, lacquered and when hard, polished with the lathe running at moderate speed.

Next, the base assembly was turned true on its upper surface and a hole $\frac{1}{2}$" diameter drilled through from the tailstock end to receive the stem cylinder end.

The ends of the stem cylinder were turned to make a push fit in the holes of bowl and base and the three components glued together under slight pressure in a bench vise.

A mandrel (plug) with a shoulder was turned on a screw flange chuck to make a snug but not force-fit in the mouth of the bowl for a depth of 3/4" and the tailstock center engaged in the existing center hole of the stem dowel, arranged to project a little beyond the bottom surface of the base. It was then a simple, straightforward routine to turn the profile of the goblet and sand, lacquer and polish it. The final act was to part off the surplus dowel end while supporting the base with the left hand as the last little pimple was ticked off and sanded smooth.

PLATE 17

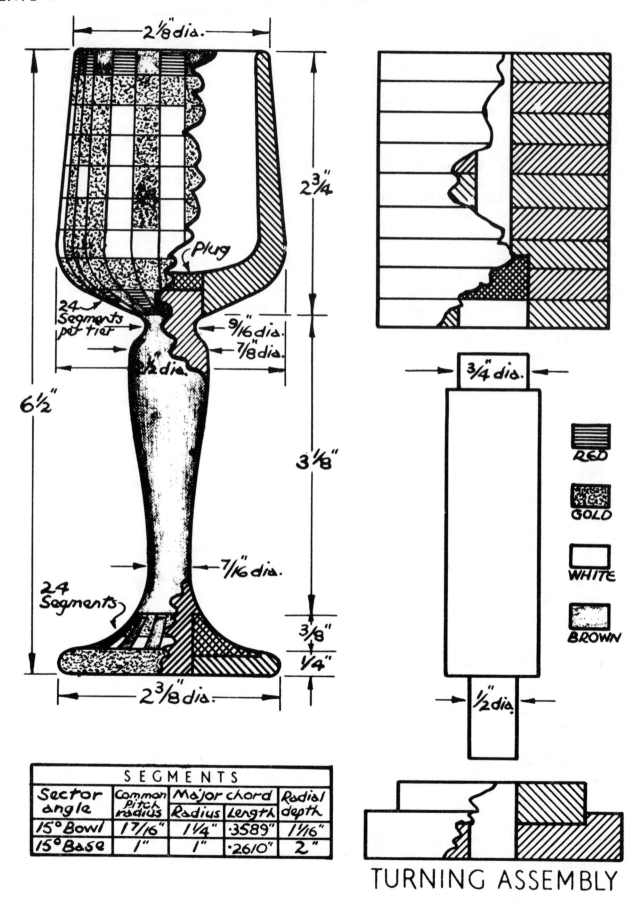

2⅛"dia.

2¾"

Plug

24 Segments per tier

9/16"dia.
7/8"dia.

½"dia.

6½"

3⅛"

7/16"dia.

24 Segments

3/8"
¼"

2⅜"dia.

¾"dia.

½"dia.

RED
GOLD
WHITE
BROWN

SEGMENTS				
Sector angle	Common pitch radius	Major chord		Radial depth
		Radius	Length	
15° Bowl	1 7/16"	1¼"	·3589"	1 1/16"
15° Base	1"	1"	·2610"	2"

TURNING ASSEMBLY

SEGMENTED GOBLET
Actual size

SEGMENTED TABLE LAMP
Plate 18

When we decided to prepare drawings of typical polychromatic articles produced during our experiments we automatically included a Table Lamp Standard because most wood turners eventually get around to making one.

Previously, the only polychromatic examples we had seen were fashioned from spindle forms of blocking with appearances that were novel, colorful (sometimes garish) and not always domestically popular. Our segmented one was an attempt to blend a mosaic kind of assembly with plain turnery and woods that were complementary in hues and working properties. There are four decorative features employed in our example: a small segmented ring at the top of the standard; a checkered, thrice repeated motif, in the main body of the stem contained in eleven rings; another small ring at its root and a broad, deep ring in the base; assemblies of 16, 24, and 24 segments respectively.

Long experience had warned us that tall, slender turnery was subject to considerable risk of fracture in normal domestic service when single plane glue lines were present. Thus our principal components were provided with dowels, shoulders or recesses to strengthen the final assembly.

The base was turned on a faceplate from a solid 1½" thick disc and given a deep shoulder and slight recess to accommodate its segment ring. The segment was turned on a separate faceplate and glued in place immediately after fitting to avoid any distortion which might soon occur and impair the quality of the glue line. A 7/8" diameter hole for the stem dowel was drilled from the tailstock end before the work was transferred to the drill press to bore a 5/16" diameter hole to admit the flexible wiring from perimeter to dowel hole via a selected segment, the outer end of which was tapped with a 3/8" thread in readiness for a plastic bushing. The base was then returned to the lathe for its final sanding and left on the faceplate. (PLATE 18, photograph 37).

The rings for the main stem decoration were accurately drilled in their centers and glue assembled in a bench vise upon a length of ½" diameter dowel in pairs, fours, etc. and as the column grew, special attention was given to secure the best vertical alignment of the pattern pieces. Next day the rough cylinder was turned to a diameter of 2 3/4" and the ends bored for the 7/8" diameter dowels of the enclosing upper and lower stem parts. These were first turned as one 2 3/4" diameter cylinder then parted proportionately. The lower part was rechucked and dowels turned to fit the holes in the main stem decoration and lamp base. The upper part was also rechucked, dowelled and recessed in the top to receive a small segment ring then glued in place.

The final assembly of the stem was executed on the lathe using the 3 jaw chuck to grip the root dowel as the components were glued, registered and placed under initial pressure by the tailstock center. After a check for grain compatibility and snug glue lines, increased pressure over a larger area was obtained by removing the tailstock center and advancing the end of the barrel. Later, the profile of the stem was turned and sanded between centers, and a 5/16"

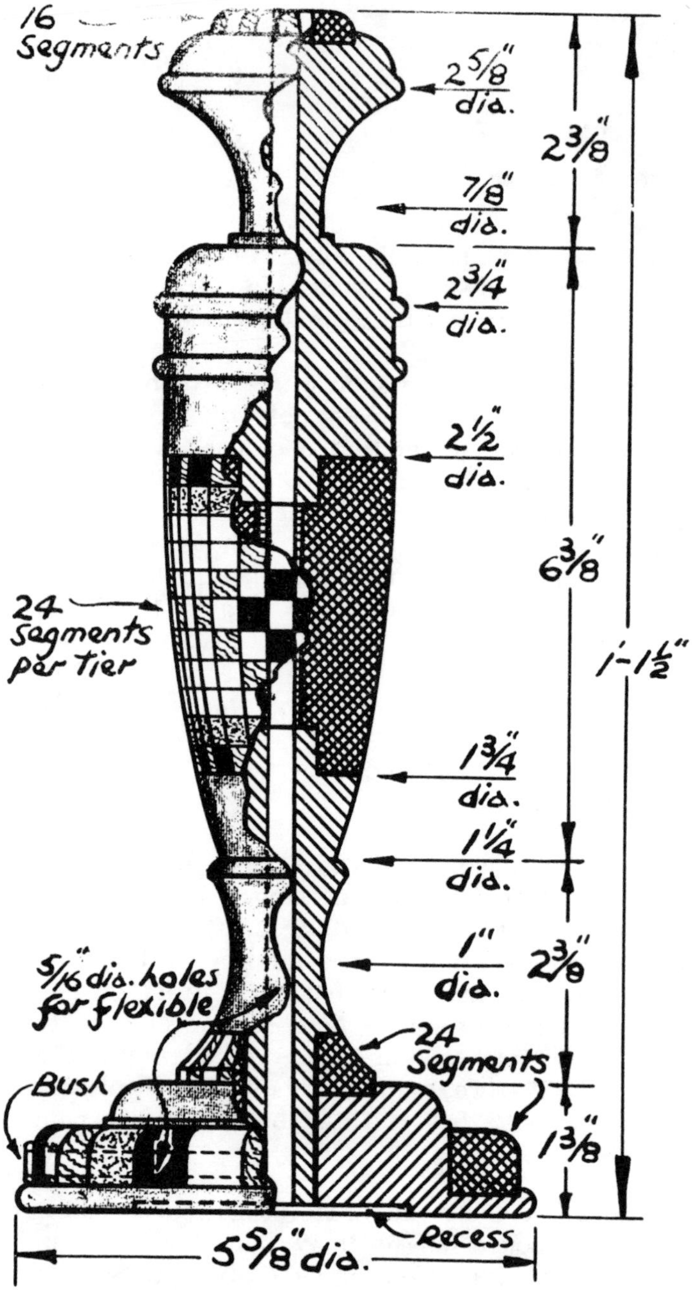
16 Segments
2 5/8" dia.
2 3/8"
7/8" dia.
2 3/4" dia.
2 1/2" dia.
6 3/8"
24 segments per tier
1'-1 1/2"
1 3/4" dia.
1 1/4" dia.
1" dia.
2 3/8"
5/16" dia. holes for flexible
24 Segments
Bush
1 3/8"
Recess
5 5/8" dia.

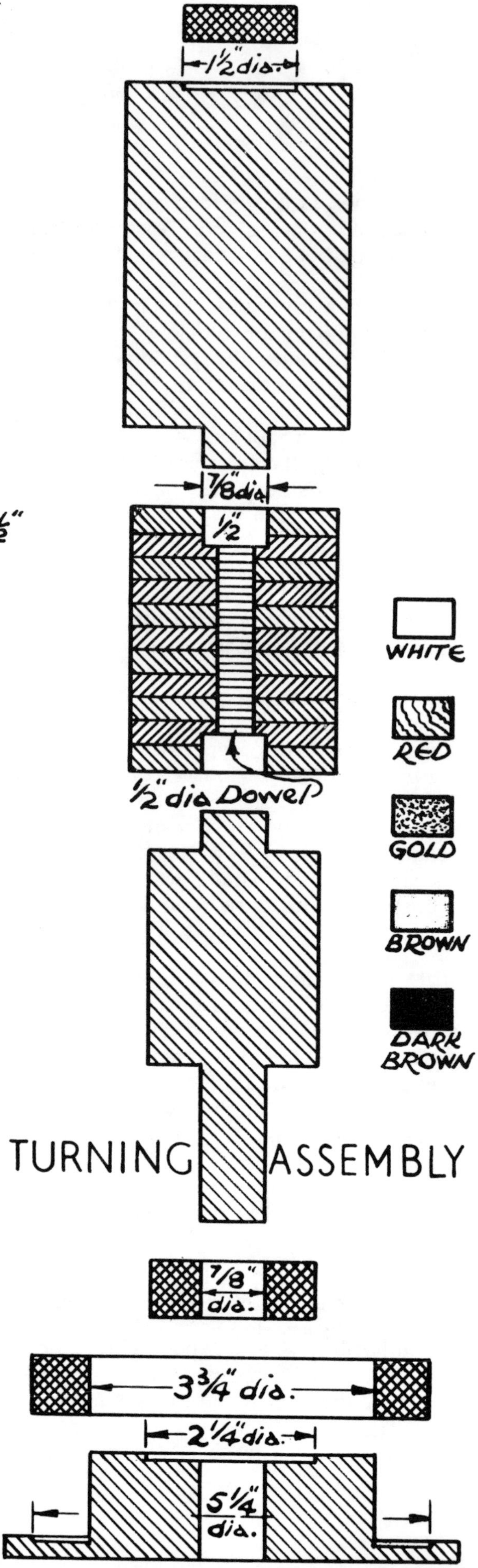
1 1/2" dia.
7/8" dia.
1/2"
1/2" dia Dowel
WHITE
RED
GOLD
BROWN
DARK BROWN
7/8" dia.
3 3/4" dia.
2 1/4" dia.
5 1/4" dia.

TURNING ASSEMBLY

SEGMENTS				
Sector angle	Common pitch radius	Major chord		Radial depth
		Radius	Length	
22½° Top	7/16"	7/8"	·3414"	7/8"
15° Centre	3/4"	1 3/8"	·3589"	1¼"
15° Bottom	19/32"	1 3/16"	·3099"	1 3/16"
15° Base	2¼"	2¾"	·7178"	1"

330 COMPONENTS

SEGMENTED TABLE LAMP

Half actual size

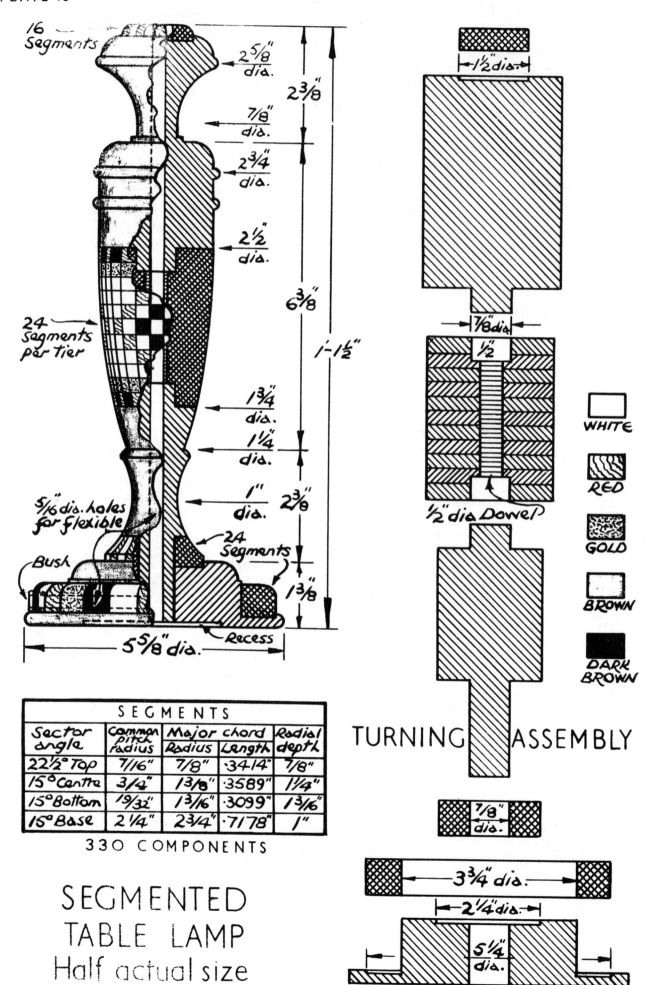

diameter hole for the wiring was bored halfway from each end on the drill press, an operation that can be safely performed on the lathe if a boring jig and long shell auger are available. The top of this hole was tapped to receive a brass lampholder nipple.

Polishing and burnishing was carried out on the lathe after many thin coats of a transparent plastic lacquer had been applied by brush at suitable intervals and allowed to harden for several days. For this operation, the base was returned to its faceplate and the stem registered by the root dowel and supported at the other end by the tailstock center running true in the nipple.

Considerable care must be observed when cutting down a lacquered surface with "Wet & Dry" abrasive paper to avoid exposing bare wood at the corners and the fine details of the assembly. Faults usually require a general levelling of the immediate area and fresh build-up of lacquer to produce a satisfactory finish.

PLATE 19

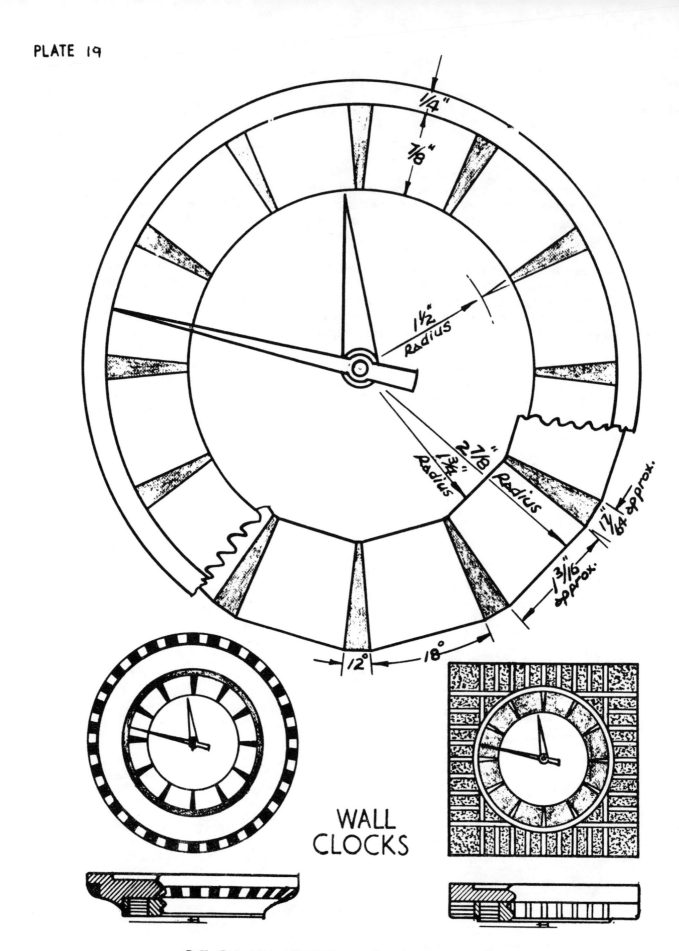

1/4"

7/8"

1½"
Radius

7/8"

1¾"
Radius

Radius

1½"
64 approx.

1 3/16"
approx.

12°

18°

WALL
CLOCKS

SEGMENTED CLOCK DIAL
Actual size

SEGMENTED CLOCK DIAL
Plate 19

It is surprising that so few examples of clocks with segmented dials are present in the multitude of designs always available on the sales counters of our leading shops and stores. The flush surface dial without numerals as presented by this form of wood construction, suffers little from extended wear and tear and only requires dusting and an occasional wipe with a damp cloth or maybe an application of furniture polish to keep it spick and span throughout the probable life of a clock movement. Segmented dials seldom spring joints or develop surface flaws as with veneered faces and the inherent simplicity of their design is surely in keeping with modern trend.

Compared with some of the polychromatic assemblies we have already described this segmented clock dial was a simple exercise. The ring contained 24 segments in alternating colors and woods, having sector angles of 12 and 18 degrees, the smaller one springing from a circle with a radius of $1\frac{1}{2}$" instead of the customary center point in order to sharpen the appearance of the hour component. (PLATE 19, photograph 42).

As we did not require many dials, the dimensions of the segments were not calculated but scaled from the full size drawing from which the miter gauge settings were also taken. Several dummy runs with scrap material were necessary before the second and larger segment sawbench set-up was arranged to deliver segments that ganged perfectly with the smaller ones to produce the required assembly diameter. We were then very pleased by its appearance and able to reproduce it in several satisfactory combinations of contrasting woods.

Rough ring assemblies were converted into accurate dials upon the disc turning holder shown on PLATE 5 and then fitted with inner discs and outer rings of solid wood, the meeting edges having a pitch of 3° to ensure hairline joints when glued and assembled, after which both surfaces were turned flat.

Various designs of wall and standing clock cases were fitted with these dials, some having polychromatic features like those shown on PLATE 19 and others - of solid, figured wood, equipped with battery or electric clock movements.

It was usually necessary to mount these cases upon a faceplate with enclosing margins in order to turn or bore cavities and sometimes recesses to receive the clock movements, then reverse the cases to seat their faces. The lacquering and polishing was executed at any convenient stage of assembly.

PLATE 20

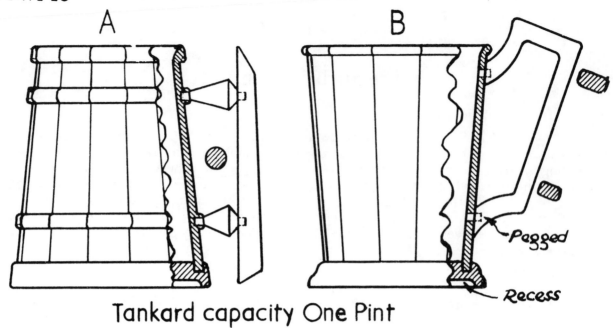

A B

Tankard capacity One Pint

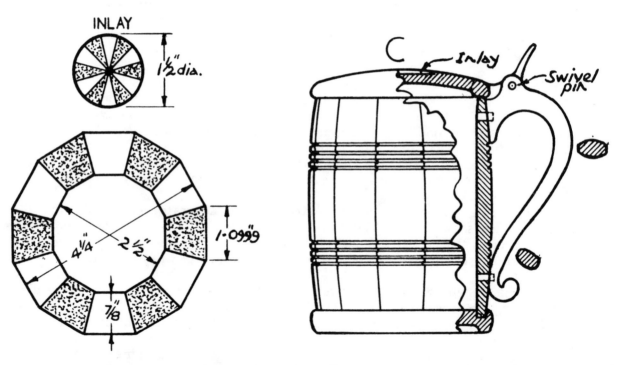

INLAY

1½"dia.

C

Inlay

Swivel pin

Pegged

Recess

4¼" 2½"

1·0999"

7/8"

SEGMENTS					TANKARDS			
Sector angle	Common pitch radius	Major chord		Radial depth	Length	Internal sizes	A	B	C
		Radius	Length						
						Max. dia	3⁵/₈"	3⁵/₈"	—
30° Staves	1¹¹/₁₆"	2¹/₈"	1·0999"	7/8"	4¹¹/₁₆"	Mean dia.	3³/₁₆"	3³/₁₆"	3³/₁₆"
30° Inlay	7/16"	7/8"	·3529"	7/8"	⅛"deep	Min. dia.	2¾"	2¾"	—
Alternate light & dark segments, total 12						Height	4½"	4½"	4½"

SEGMENTED TANKARDS
Half actual size

SEGMENTED TANKARDS
Plate 20

Wooden drinking vessels are now regarded as museum or collectors items and their centuries of service as a principal form of utensil for convivial beverage are almost forgotten in the abundance of elegant receptacles now available in ceramics, glass, fine metals and plastics.

Past polychromatic specimens were usually of the staved, feathered and coopered variety which had a relatively short functional life due to the permeable nature of wood, then sometimes coated with pitch and varnishes not able to offer the standard of protection attained by modern synthetic lacquers.

We consider that any representative collection of polychromatic turnery should include an example of cylindrical segmentation, a logical method for the construction of tankards required for decorative or more practical purposes. PLATE 20 shows three typical patterns, each with a capacity of one Imperial Pint (20 oz. in US).

For cylindrical assemblies we cut the segment strips lengthwise from boards thicknessed to the radial depth, using the sliding carrier, hinged fence and canted table or tilted saw arrangements shown on PLATES 2, 3 and 4. It was possible to dispense with the first two aids and use the ripfence when the strips were long enough to be pushed past the saw in a smooth operation. These strips were crosscut to job length and assembled in alternate wood species and colors with three band clamps and when the adhesive was set, the ends were levelled square against a disc sander. Next, a mandrel was turned which made a push fit with the tangent points of the cylinder interior and wedges were inserted at the ends to prevent lateral movement while the exterior surface was turned into a true cylinder. This was transferred to a self centering chuck for hollowing and shaping one end to fit into the base.

A sawn disc 1" thick was used for this base, screwed to a faceplate and turned $\frac{1}{4}$" larger than its final diameter with a groove that made a push fit over the bottom rim of the cylinder, then glued in place without removing the faceplate by which means it was possible to complete the hollowing of the assembly with side and corner chisels, followed by sanding off. At this stage we usually prefer to complete the interior by applying clear, waterproof lacquer in three series of triple coats, flattened and finished off as described previously for other projects.

To facilitate the exterior shaping, a plug was turned on a faceplate to fit loosely inside the mouth of the cylinder, the slack being made up with self adhesive paper and the base supported by the tailstock center. Thus the work was held securely and without vibration or damage to the lacquered surface as the barrel was reduced to its final shape, the thickness of the staves being checked by withdrawing the assembly from the plug. (Photograph 37).

The screw holes in the base were removed as it was parted off to the design depth, leaving a central pip until the external sanding, lacquering and polishing was virtually complete. Then the tailstock was withdrawn and the toolrest placed across and close to the bottom surface while the recess was turned out. All further sanding and polishing was executed without help from the toolrest or tailstock as the work was held safely enough by the plug and sensible manual support.

Handles for tankards are nearly always shapely without loss of comfort or strength to survive moderate domestic hazards but we must confess to the use of a somewhat delicate form of attachment as we hope to keep our specimens under temperate surveillance.

The handle for tankard "A" comprises of three turned parts assembled by integral dowels and drillings. Those for the other tankards were sawn from selected flat, tapered stock which was carved, filed and sanded into cross sections that felt comfortable. The "C" pattern was forked to receive a matching leaf and thumblift fitted to the lid, to provide a hinge.

Seatings for handles can be arranged by making flats on the staves and roots of the handles but we preferred to shape the roots to match the barrel curvatures. This was achieved by turning discs of the same diameters as the barrels at points of attachment, around which we glued abrasive cloth and then ground the roots to the exact concave shapes. The tricky job was to drill the dowel holes in the correct places before bedding and attachment with strong resin adhesive.

The lid of tankard "C" was embellished with a segmented inlay.

PLATE 21

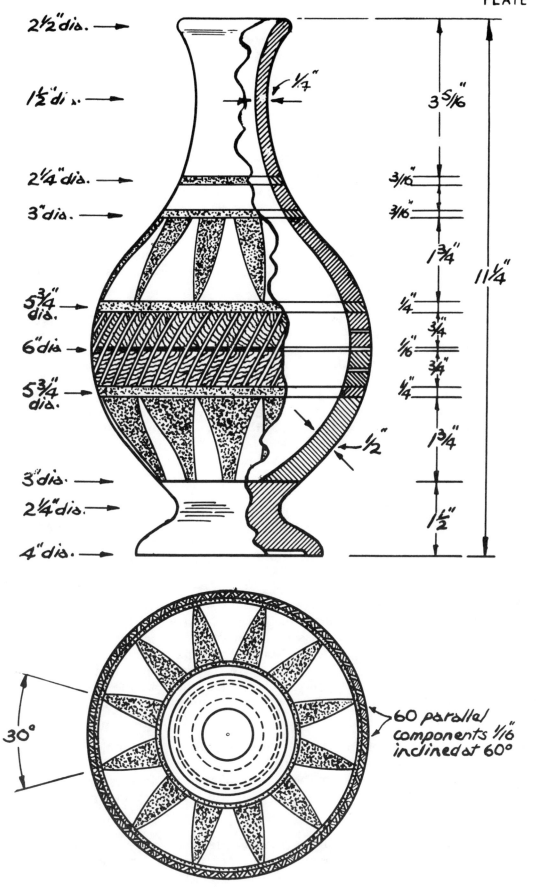

2½"dia.

1½"dia.

¼"

3⁵/₁₆"

2¼"dia.

3"dia.

3/16"

3/16"

1¾"

5¾" dia.

¼"

6"dia.

¾"

1/16"

5¾" dia.

¾"

¼"

3"dia.

1¾"

2¼"dia.

½"

4"dia.

½"

11¼"

30°

60 parallel
components 1/16"
inclined at 60°

SEGMENTED VASE
Half actual size

SEGMENTED VASE
Plate 21

Large, free standing ornaments are seldom turned in solid wood because it is difficult to obtain stock of suitable dimensions with good appearance and the essential stability. Also, the hollowing process usually requires deep boring equipment, a heavy lathe and turning ability not easily acquired or sought by nervous craftsmen.

By using polychromatic assemblies turned in stages it is possible to construct hollow vases of considerable size provided that sound sawing, assembly and turning methods are employed.

So far, the majority of components used in the projects described were produced by circular saw whereas the chief decorative features of the vase shown on PLATE 21 were freely bandsawn from tiered discs of contrasting softwoods, the segments alternating in second assemblies to achieve a petal band effect.

The central decorative band is comprised of two similar discs with edge grain reversed. This is separated by a thin layer of another wood, slotted with a 60° inclination by bandsaw to admit contrasting wood strips. This assembly was then levelled on the top and bottom surfaces for the attachment of further wood layers. The components for the narrow neck were assembled in one simple press operation.

Next, the solid base, lower petal band and central band were joined, mounted on a faceplate and hollowed with hand turning tools, using an internal template to ensure that an adequate wall thickness was left. The upper petal band was hollowed on another faceplate, then released and attached to the major assembly retained on the first faceplate.

The neck assembly was hollowed by gripping it in a 3 jaw chuck, using a drill advanced by the tailstock. The top end of the bore was fitted with a plug having an overlapping flange to facilitate final assembly on the lathe, using the tailstock to press the neck against the main assembly on the faceplate, thus aligning the work accurately between centers. It was then easy to shape the outside of the vase. The plug was removed and the toolrest placed just clear of the neck cavity to complete the rim and blend the inside profile into the main body of the vase.

All polishing was executed on the lathe, first by adding many thin coats of clear synthetic lacquer by brush and hand rotation, cutting down after each third coat with abrasives and the lathe in motion until a smooth, level surface was obtained. This was burnished into a high glaze and then eased back to a more durable glow.

Other fine examples of large hollow turnery devised and made by Mr. Larralde appear in PLATES 31-33 some of which were hollowed by deep boring equipment, but in the main they were constructed by the methods we have described, using attractive wood species with good color contrasts and grain patterns. Being decorative rather than utilitarian in character it was not considered necessary to use shouldered or tongued joints as the adhesives employed were usually stronger than the fibers of the woods they combined.

PLATE 22

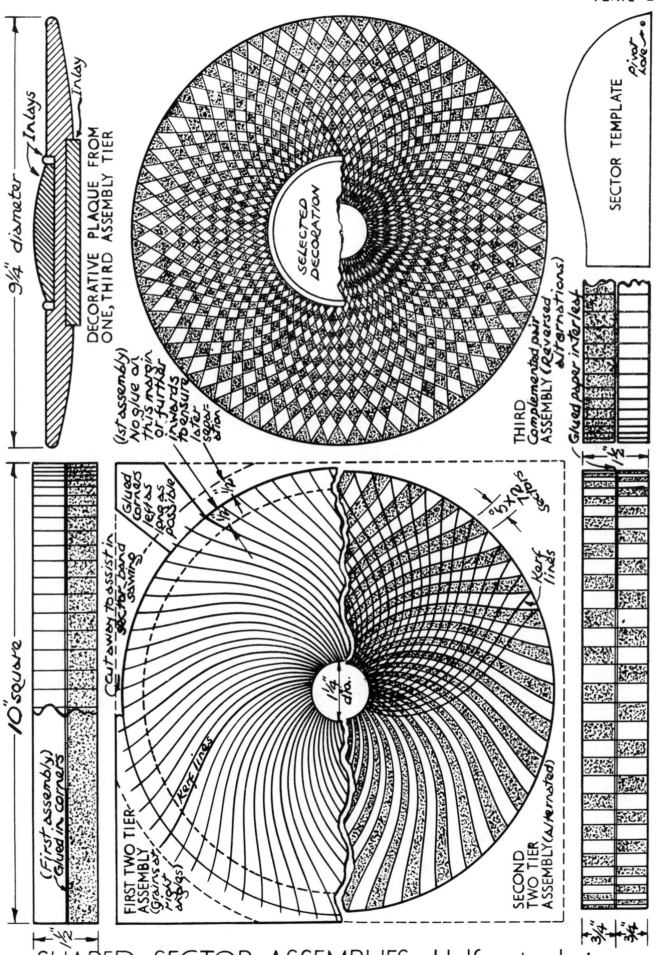

9¼" diameter

Inlays

Inlay

DECORATIVE PLAQUE FROM ONE, THIRD ASSEMBLY TIER

SECTOR TEMPLATE

pivot hole

SELECTED DECORATION

THIRD
Complemented pair
ASSEMBLY (Reversed
alternations)

Glued paper interleaf

½"

(1st assembly)
No glue at
this margin
or further
inwards
to ensure
later separ-
ation

Glued
corners
left as
long as
possible

Cut away to assist in
sector-band sawing

Kerf lines

¹⁄₁₆" x ¹⁄₁₆" sectors

Kerf lines

1¼" dia.

FIRST TWO TIER
ASSEMBLY
(Grains at
right angles)

SECOND
TWO TIER
ASSEMBLY (Alternated)

10" square

(First assembly)
Glued in corners

½"

3/8"   ¾"

SHAPED SECTOR ASSEMBLIES - Half actual size

SHAPED SECTOR ASSEMBLIES

Plate 22

Some of the most original and pleasing polychromatic patterns shown in the Plates of executed turnery are assemblies of shaped sectors bandsawn from two tiered stock rearranged with alternating wood hues.

PLATE 22 (Photographs 34 & 58) shows a typical zebra pattern produced by this method which can be converted into a smaller diamond pattern by a further sawing and assembly which doubles the number of components and complexity of the design, not as difficult to achieve as the drawing might suggest. Both patterns can be extracted from two squares of contrasting woods, preferably plain and assembled in tier with grains at right angles to each other, using glued paper interleaf in the corners and a limited central area.

The zebra pattern is marked on the upper surface of the lighter wood, using a template which pivots in the exact center of the square, ascertained by striking the diagonals. It registers with 5° intervals on the inscribed disc perimeter determined by protractor or other accurate means and is best made in a thin, rigid, transparent material which reveals the emerging pattern as the marking out proceeds and helps to avoid fractional errors in sector widths. All sectors are numbered in rotation and a hole about $1\frac{1}{4}$" diameter is drilled through the center of the assembly, then bandsawn into quadrants with corners cut clear on both sides and disc outline to give immediate access for sector bandsawing, the corners being left for handling comfort until the last sectors are reached. Numbering is then repeated on the bottom and both tiers of the sectors before they are separated and reassembled in alternating species and strict order by means of band clamps, these discs being complementary.

The diamond pattern is produced by assembling a pair of zebra discs in tier with levelled surfaces, glued paper interleaf and sector lines and numbers matched on their edges. The central hole is given a temporary plug in which to establish a new pivot center for the template while another set of sectors are marked out from existing 5° intervals but in reverse direction. The plug is then removed and the assembly quartered before individual sectors are bandsawn and reassembled in alternating tier rotation, using band clamps. Perfect registration of components and sector outlines in this assembly can not be expected but interstices should be rare and easily made good with matching fillers to give a finished appearance regulated but not dominated by its geometric character.

In the drawing on PLATE 22, the innermost area of the diamond pattern assembly has been deliberately given an uneven appearance to illustrate the need for a fairly large, separate center decoration because it is beyond normal manual limits of bandsawing to preserve symmetrical outlines in fine patterns as they approach the disc center.

Delicate patterns can be introduced into plain discs by bandsawing sectors and outlining them with strips of contrasting veneer equal in thickness to the saw kerf, assembling by band clamps.

FAMILY GOBLETS
Plate 22A

To commemorate auspicious royal, national and international events it is customary for many manufacturers of drinking vessels to produce souvenir designs, the best in limited numbers to become collectors pieces.

As a juvenile attending Council School I received a George V & Mary Coronation Mug and another to mark the peace celebrations for the First World War. In a family with ten children who took turns at washing, up these ceramic mugs were short lived. Tankards awarded for success in field sports during bachelor years became so battered that it was considered prudent to lose them at marriage rather than test the goodwill of a houseproud spouse.

It needed the sight of a "Moon Landing" souvenir goblet, a surplus of attractive polychromatic segment rings and survival into retirement to induce me to design and make a set of four inscribed with two generations of family cyphers as detailed below.

CYPHER	PERSON	GOBLET WOOD	
CB	Self	Masur Birch	Limba, Tangile, Vinhatico
VB	Wife	English Yew	African Padauk, Claro Walnut
IRB	Son	Wild Cherry	Cigarbox Cedar, Prima Vera
MB	Daughter-in-law	London Plane	American Holly, Black Walnut

All these goblets were 5¼" high with bowl and base diameters varying between 4" to 2½", wall and stem dimensions being more robust than those made in conventional materials but without making their appearance clumsy or weight excessive. They were turned from well seasoned stock 7" long into cylinders with slightly concave ends and poppet holes left to register other stages of the work.

The general turning procedure was similar for each goblet, commenced by mounting the cylinder on a flange chuck with diameter less than the base of the vessel, using a No. 20 central woodscrew and three No. 8 woodscrews near the rim for extra stability. Then, with the tailstock center engaged, the cylinder was skimmed to correct any eccentricity caused by mounting before a shoulder was turned at the tailstock end by parting tool and scraping chisel to seat the bowl segment ring with a slip fit, or when the bowl shape so required, in half rings, glued in place immediately to avoid possible warping. The segment ring blank was mounted by double-sided self-adhesive tape on to a turned disc, held by a 3 jaw self-centering chuck when being opened to fit the shoulder seating.

The bowl cavity was formed by boring a pilot hole with a 1" diameter center bit advanced by the tailstock and opened out by a round nosed scraping tool, using a card template to check the shape, taking care not to remove the bit lead hole required to locate the recess for a segmented disc inlay. This recess was made by a Forstner bit to secure a flat bottom and the inlay glued in place with the top 1/8" proud of the surrounding surface, using the barrel of the tailstock as a press. Surplus inlay was turned out as the cavity was completed and sanded with the rim turnover, then sealed and bodied up with brush coats of clear, waterproof lacquer applied in series of three and when hard cut down with "Wet & Dry", and burnished to a high glaze with the lathe in motion.

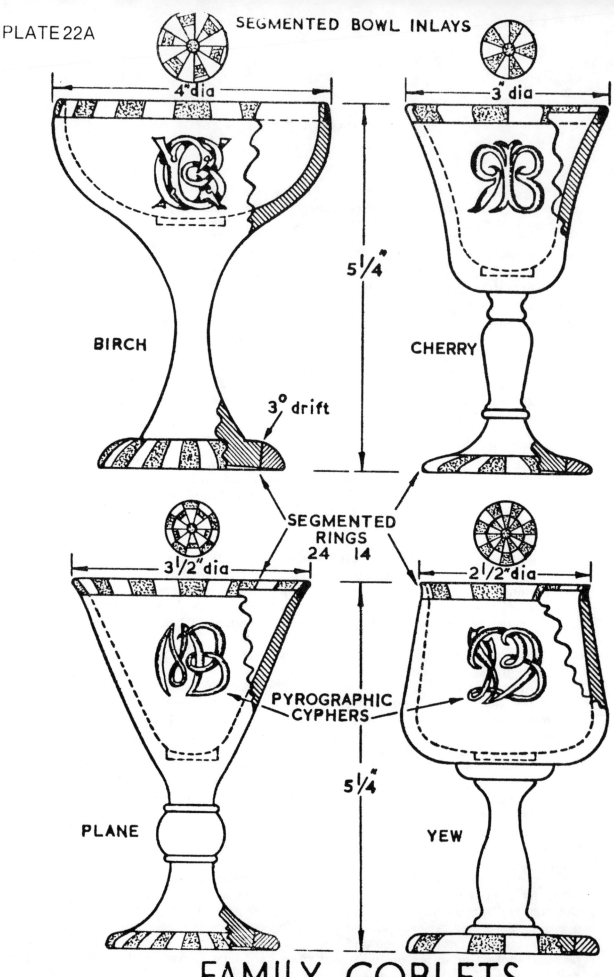

PLATE 22A

SEGMENTED BOWL INLAYS

4"dia

3" dia

5¼"

BIRCH

CHERRY

3° drift

SEGMENTED
RINGS
24   14

3½"dia

2½"dia

PYROGRAPHIC
CYPHERS

PLANE

YEW

5¼"

FAMILY GOBLETS
¾ actual size

April, 1975

To facilitate the external shaping a block of waste wood was securely mounted on a flange chuck and turned into a plug which matched the upper part of the bowl cavity with a loose fit. Slack was made up with evenly distributed layers of self-adhesive drafting tape, the tailstock center registered in the base poppet hole and judicious pressure applied to seat the cavity firmly over the plug with enough overlap to prevent it from springing out during turning operations. It was necessary to remove the workpiece from the plug several times to check the thickness of the bowl wall but it reseated perfectly and no dangerous movements occurred once the bowl settled on the resilient packing. Although not essential I used a loose tailstock center and as the turning proceeded, increased the pressure several times to eliminate fractional creep.

The base of the goblet was turned with a 3° drift to wedge the counterpart seating of its segment ring and when glued a parting cut $\frac{1}{2}$" deep was made to define the bottom surface. After sanding, the cypher outline was added by carbon paper impression, inscribed by pyrography, infilled by pigments that matched the segmentation and the entire external surface lacquer finished as described for the interior.

Parting the remaining waste from the base was the critical part of the job, executed with maximum caution to within $\frac{1}{4}$" of separation, completed by a fine saw cut with the lathe at rest. Then the toolrest was placed across and close to the bottom surface to turn this slightly concave with scraping tool tickles, sanded smooth and endorsed with the date and wood name by pyrography before sealing with lacquer.

The goblet had then become a family heirloom prospect.

SEGMENTED BOWL IN STAR PATTERN
Plate 22B

This striking example of polychromatic turnery was extracted from a glued assembly comprised of three main parts, rim, body and base, using four different woods.

The rim was a simple six segment ring 10" in diameter cut from a planed strip of maple 1" wide X 3/8" thick upon a circular sawbench with the sliding miter gauge set at 30°, the components being assembled by band clamp.

For the body, two planed discs of contrasting woods 9" diameter. X 2" thick were assembled by glued paper interleaf and a star pattern marked on top and bottom surfaces with twelve corresponding points connected by vertical edge lines. The segments between the star fingers were similarly numbered on all surfaces in sequence then cut out by bandsaw, taking care to make the kerfs meet perfectly and vertical. All components were then separated and reassembled in the same sequence except for tier alternation to obtain discs in two woods and colors, with their surfaces planed level. This method produced two reversed body assemblies so it was logical to make a pair of bowls.

The base was a planed, bandsawn disc 3" in diameter X 7/8" thick in the fourth contrasting wood.

These main parts were assembled under pressure with center points on a common vertical axis and the resulting block was screwed to a faceplate, base outwards. The exterior shape of the bowl was then turned and sanded and before release from the faceplate, brush lacquered, cut back with mild abrasives and burnished on the lathe in motion. The interior turning was accomplished with the base gripped in a felted 3 jaw self-centering chuck, hollowing by gouge and round nosed scraper to a depth where a shallow recess for the central inlay was sunk by corner chisel to the glueline of the attached base.

The inlay was a twenty-four segment assembly in three contrasting woods turned from a button blank $1\frac{1}{2}$" diameter and when glued in place the interior turning was completed and sanded.

"Davida" style capitals were used for the inscription, a quotation from Chaucer which read "THE LIFE SO SHORT-THE CRAFT SO LONG TO LEARN", transferred by carbon-paper impression from an outline layout on tracing paper, then made indelible by pyrography, infilled with dyes that harmonized with the hues of adjacent woods. The bowl interior and rim were then given several coats of lacquer and finished off to match the exterior surface.

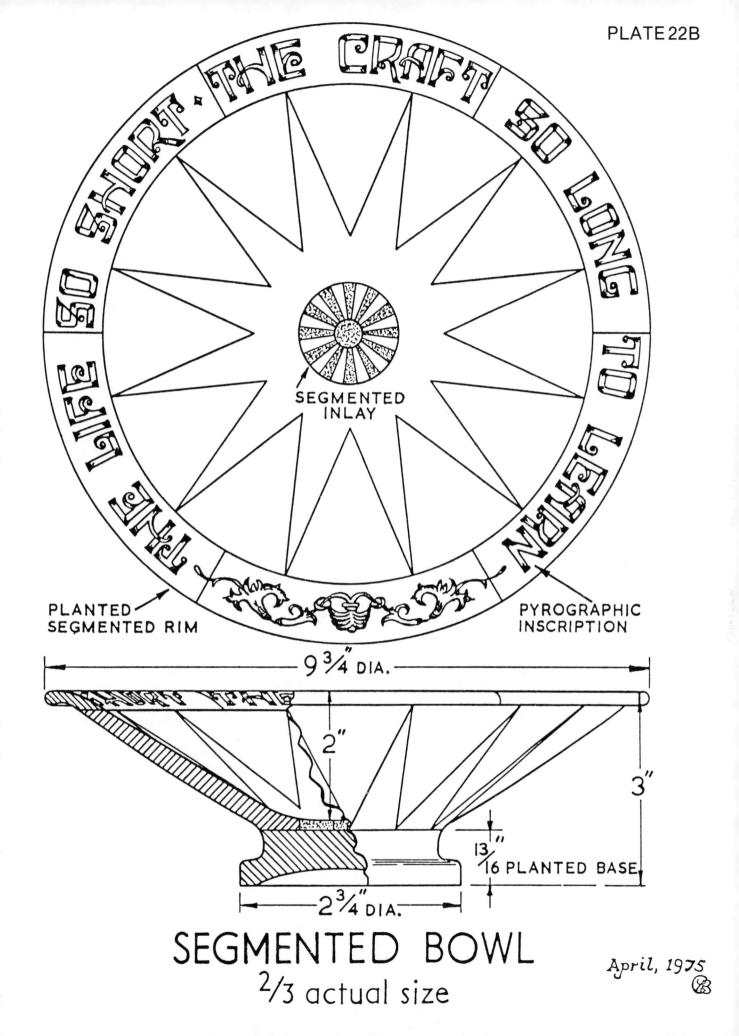

THE LIFE SO SHORT · THE CRAFT SO LONG TO LEARN

SEGMENTED INLAY

PLANTED SEGMENTED RIM

PYROGRAPHIC INSCRIPTION

9 3/4" DIA.

2"

3"

13/16" PLANTED BASE

2 3/4" DIA.

SEGMENTED BOWL
2/3 actual size

April, 1975

RECOMMENDED WOODS

No rewarding purpose can be served by presenting a schedule of wood species known to possess the ideal colors and other qualities required for satisfactory polychromatic assemblies when prospective exponents are unlikely to possess or acquire more than a few of them when commencing this kind of work. This is perhaps a good thing because it will minimize costs until the initial snags of the craft are encountered and overcome. Early experience with common, plain, inexpensive woods in good supply and a restricted color range will help to secure pleasing effects and patterns without extremes of contrast before the limits of machines and pocket are reached, leaving a margin for more ambitious assemblies.

Our wood stocks were built up by many years of search, purchase and exchange as active members of various wood and craft societies. Unless you have exceptional contacts, the will to forage, considerable wood knowledge and a deep pocket you must be content to work in a few indigenous and imported species until strips of more exotic woods have been accumulated. Fortunately, the cross sectional dimensions of the strips used for most projects are small which increases the chances of picking up job lots of uncommon woods as offcuts, short ends and left-overs from trade orders in large timber yards . . . if you can establish obliging contacts. It is almost impossible to obtain small supplies of exotic species on the open market by any other means.

The schedule which follows is arranged in fairly broad color bands aligned with the common and botanical names of woods we consider appropriate and have used to produce satisfactory assemblies over a period of fifteen years. It is offered as a record and guide but not as a specific index of the best woods available in the full range of colors covered by the commercial timbers of the world. These are often restricted to certain areas and periods of supply as trade conditions change. Many woods recommended in books written in the first half of this century are no longer available and local merchants have fewer species in stock.

Remember that the hues, markings, textures, and other properties of wood vary from plank to plank, sometimes from foot to foot and that all wood changes color, usually darker with age and exposure to light. It also loses luster and is adversely affected by deterioration in polish or lacquer, particularly so when pigmentation is used as with french polish. The use of special grain fillers may assist in obtaining a level surface quickly but we prefer to fill with extra coats of a clear body lacquer to establish a more uniform natural appearance.

And finally, remember that beautiful wood, like gold, is where you find it.

RECOMMENDED WOODS

SPECIES

COLOR	COMMON NAME	BOTANICAL NAME
BLACK	Bog Oak	Quercus
	*Ebony (various)	Diospyros
INDIGO	African Blackwood	Dalbergia melanoxylon
	American walnut	Juglans nigra
	Brazilian rosewood	Dalbergia nigra
	Indian rosewood	Dalbergia latifolia
	*Kingwood	Dalbergia cearensis
GREY	*Harewood (dyed)	Acer pseudoplatanus
	Various other mineral stained species	
PURPLE	Bubinga	Guibourtia demeusii
	*Purpleheart	Peltogyne
RED (dark)	Dark red meranti	Shorea pauciflora
	Jarrah	Eucalyptus marginata
	Burmese red cedar	Cedrela toona
	*Red sanders	Pterocarpus santalinus
(medium)	African mahogany	Khaya ivorensis
	Makore	Tieghemella heckelii
	Sapele	Entandrophragma cylindricum
	*Tangile	Shorea polysperma
	Utile	Entandrophragma utile
(orange)	*African padauk	Pterocarpus soyauxii
	Andaman padauk	Pterocarpus dalbergioides
BROWN (dark)	Australian walnut	Endiandra palmerstonii
	Black bean	Castanospermum australe
	Brown oak	Quercus robur
	*European walnut	Juglans regia
	Ipil	Intsia bijuga
	Mansonia	Mansonia altissima
(medium)	African walnut	Lovoa klaineana
	Afrormosia	Pericopsis elata
	Afzelia	Afzelia
	American mahogany	Swietenia macrophylla
	American red gum	Liquidambar styraciflua
	Butternut	Juglans cinerea
	Iroko	Chlorophora excelsa
	Koa	Acacia Koa
	Oak (various)	Quercus
	*Teak	Tectona grandis
(light)	*Beech (various)	Fagus
	Light Lauan	Pentacme contorta
	Limba	Terminalia superba
	Myrtlewood	Umbellularia californica
	Plane (various)	Platanus hybrida

RECOMMENDED WOODS

SPECIES

COLOR	COMMON NAME	BOTANICAL NAME
ORANGE (dark)	American cherry	Prunus serotina
	*English yew	Taxus baccata
	Osage orange	Maclura pomifera
(light)	Ceylon satinwood	Chloroxylon swietenia
	Opepe	Nauclea diderrchii
	Prima vera	Tabebuia donnell-smithii
	*Vinhatico	Plathymenia reticulata
YELLOW (dark)	Knysna boxwood	Gonioma kamassi
	*Maracaibo boxwood	Gossypiospermum praecox
(light)	Avodire	Turraeanthus africanus
	Birch (various)	Betula
	*Obeche	Triplochiton scleroxylon
	Podo	Podocarpus gracilior
	Ramin	Gonystylus macrophyllum
(cream)	American whitewood	Liriodendron tulipifera
	Ash (various)	Fraxinus
	*European sycamore	Acer pseudoplatanus
	Hornbeam	Carpinus betulus
	Magnolia (various)	Magnolia
	Maple (various)	Acer
	Yellow cedar	Chamaecyparis nootkatensis
WHITE (off)	*Holly (various)	Ilex
	Poplar (various)	Populus
	Various other blond species	

*Species that we consider most typical of the colors indicated which are not related to any standard chart or spectrum but are offered as a rough guide to wood hues. These are less brilliant than the customary conception of color values.

NOTE: As far as possible, the nomenclature adopted is in accordance with the Handbook of Hardwoods, 2nd edition. HMSO 1972 and Timbers of the World , TRADA, 1979.

PLATE 23

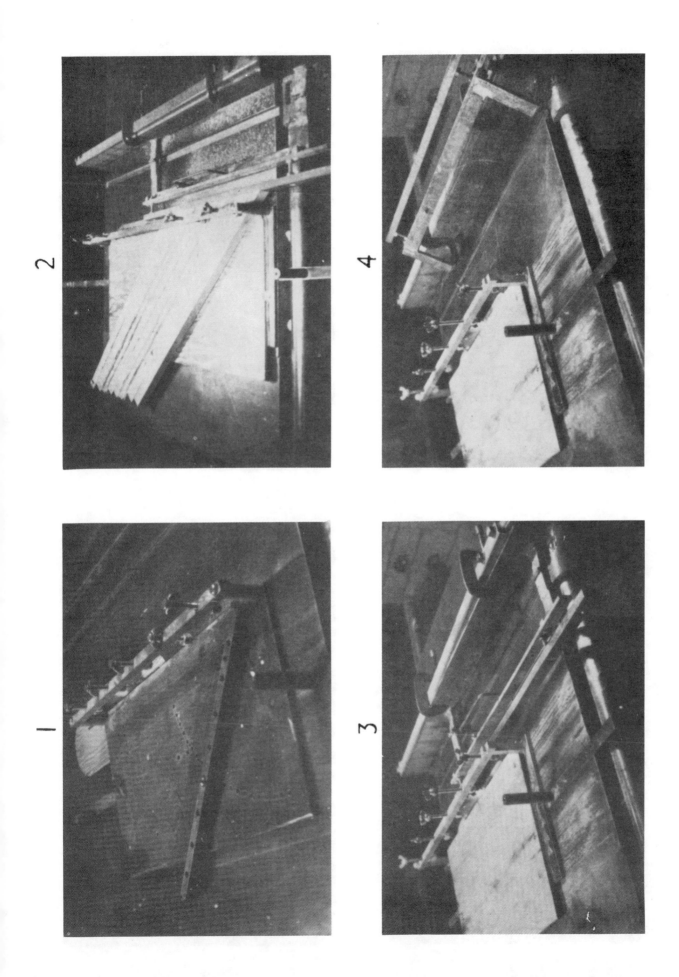

PLATE 24 -88-

6

8

5

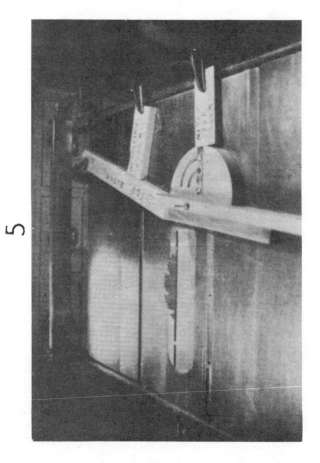

7

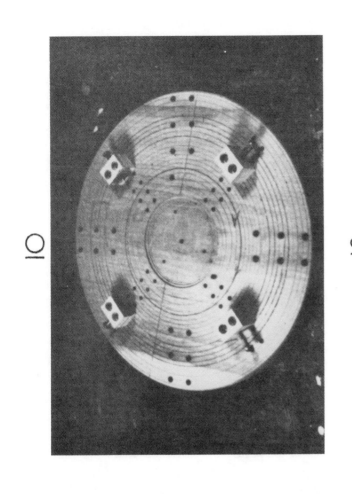

10

12

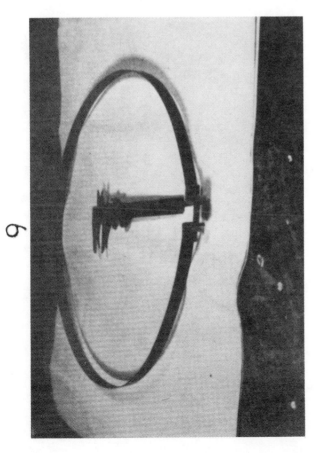

9

11

PLATE 26 -90-

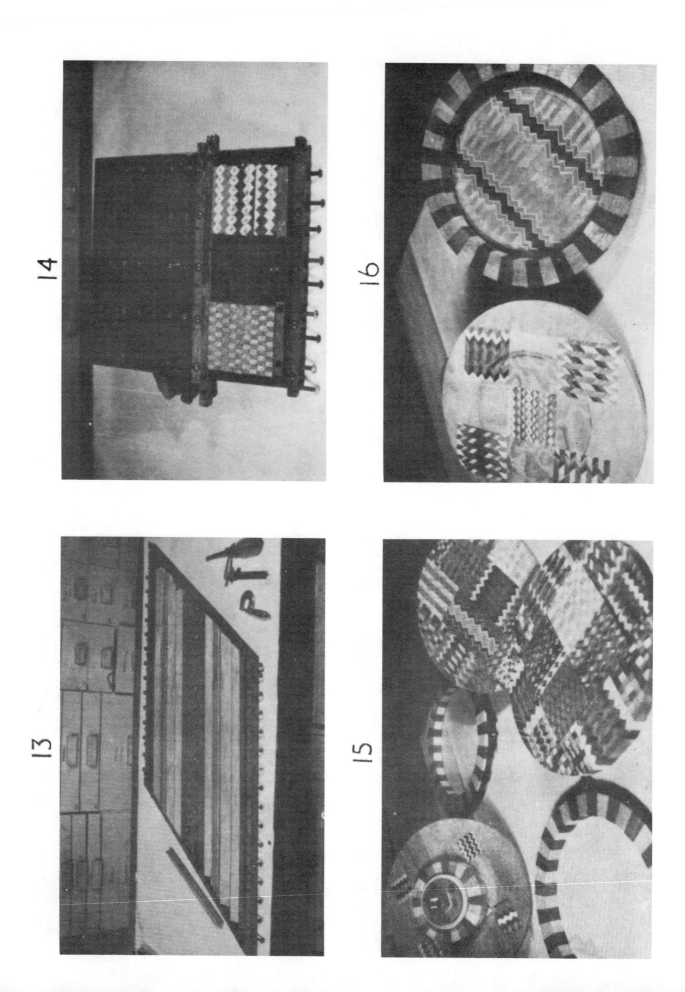

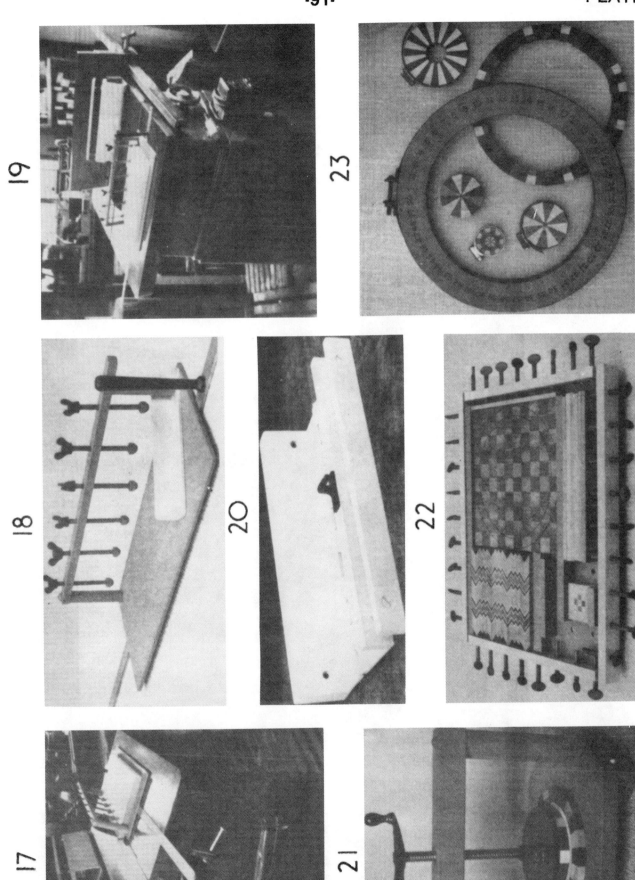

PLATE 28

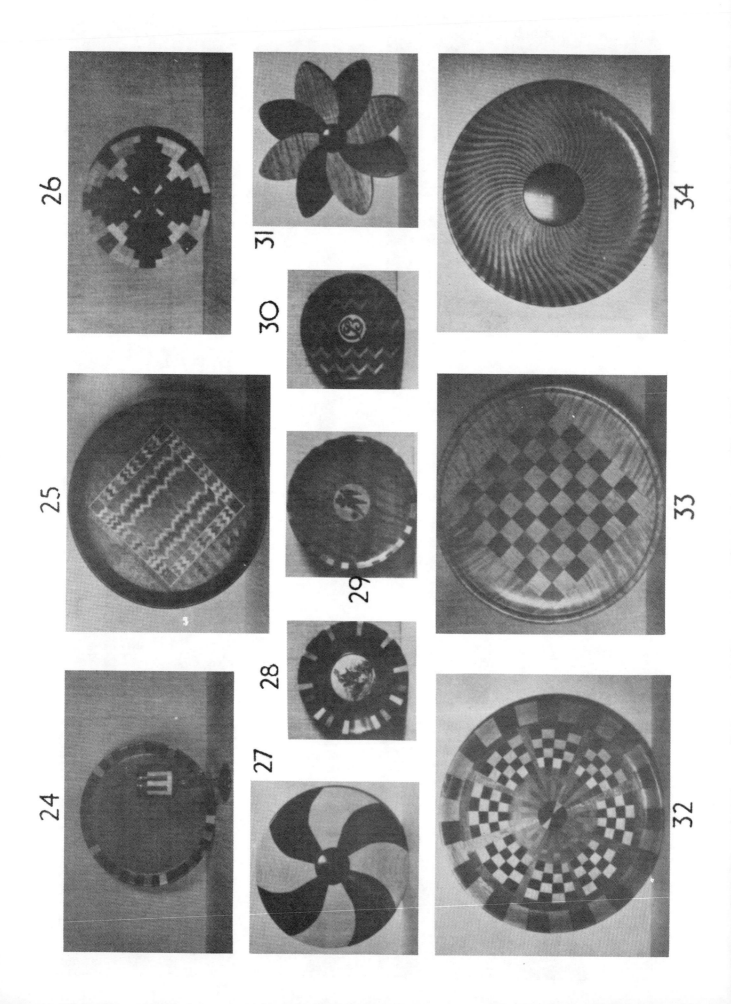

37

39

42

36

40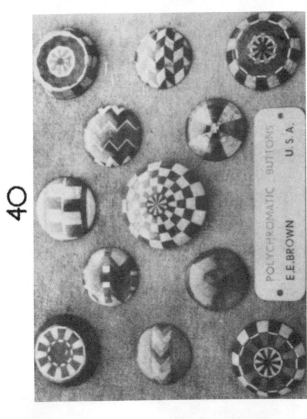

POLYCHROMATIC BUTTONS

E.E.BROWN   U.S.A.

35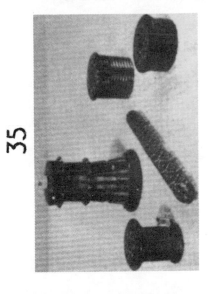

38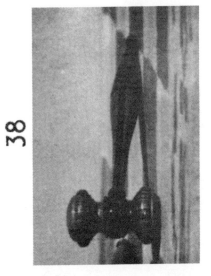

41

PLATE 30 -94-

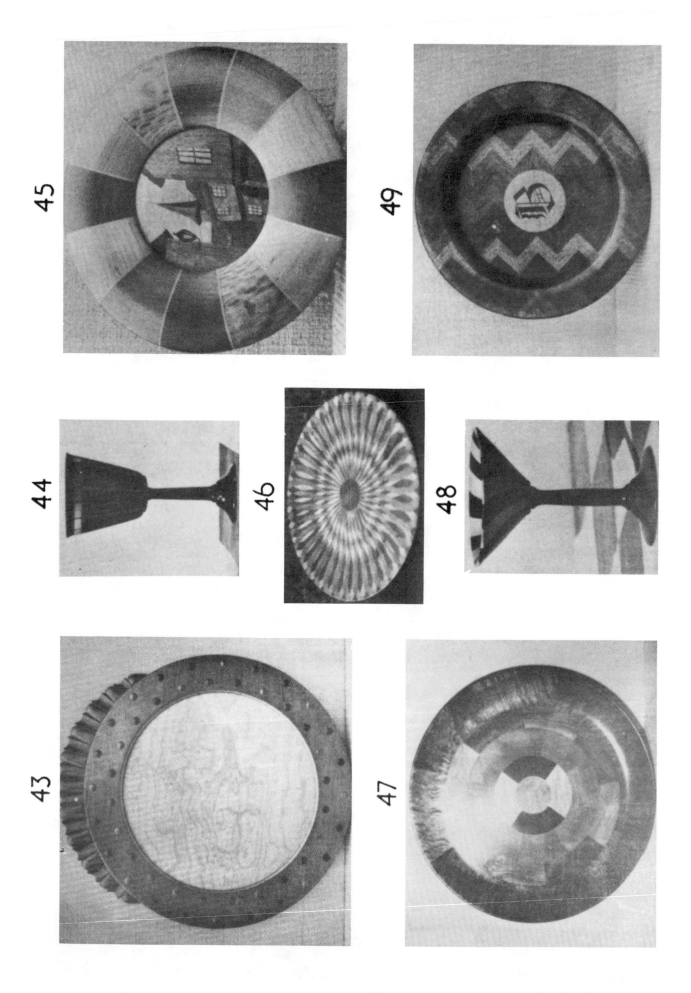

PLATE 31

50

51

52

53

56

54

55

PLATE 32

57

58

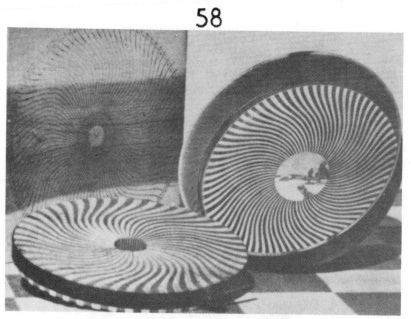

59

60

61

62

PLATE 33

65

64

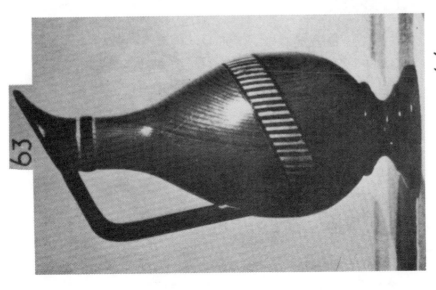

63

67

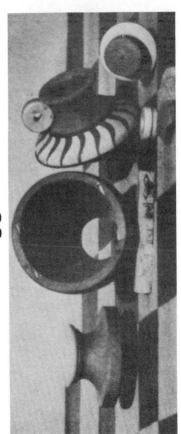

66

PLATE 34   -98-

70

73

76

69

72

75

68

71

74

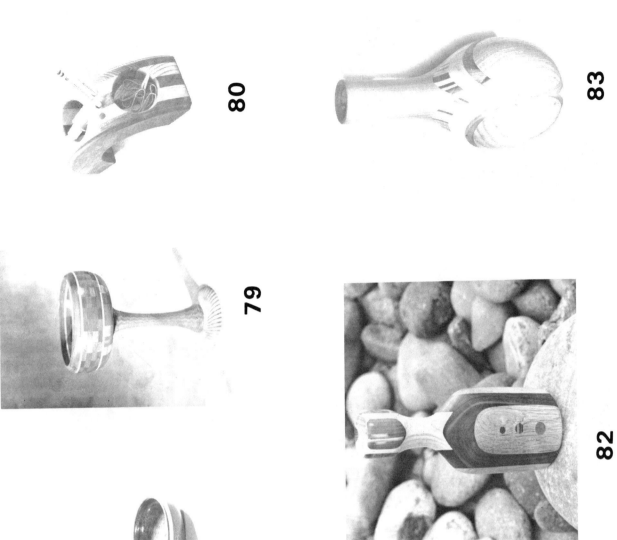

80

83

79

82

78

77

81

PLATE 36 -100-

86

89

85

88

84

87

PLATE 37

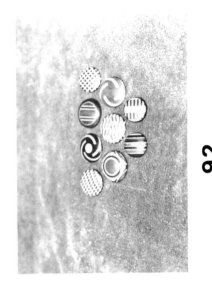

92

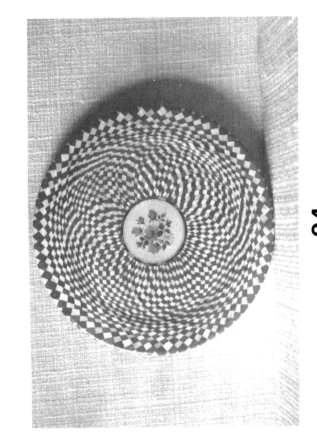

94

91

93

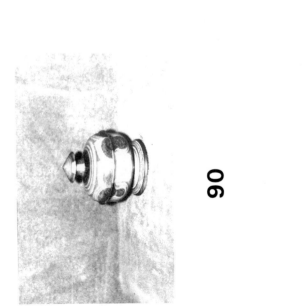

90

BIBLIOGRAPHY

The Bibliography is divided into three sections, 1) Studding, Inlaying, and Laminating; 2) Blocking, Single and Multiple, Including Cross-Lamination; 3) Segmenting, Ring and Sector, Stave Work. Each of these sections are further divided into particular references by worker and secondly to books having pertinant information to our subject.

Abbreviations:

BSOT- BULLETIN OF THE SOCIETY OF ORNAMENTAL TURNERS

FWW- FINE WOODWORKING. The Taunton Press, Box 355, Newtown CT 06470

FWWBDB-FINE WOODWORKING BIENNIAL DESIGN BOOK. 1977.

FWWDBII-FINE WOODWORKING DESIGN BOOK II 1979

GTO- A GALLERY OF TURNED OBJECTS. Albert LeCoff, ed. Brigham Young University Press. Provo, UT 1981

STUDDING, INLAYING AND LAMINATING

Alderson, William. BSOT, No. 27 (VI), Aug. 1962, P. 30. Laminated Bowl

Askey, J.S. BSOT, No. 40 (IX), March, 1969, p. 143, Plaques of polychromatic inlay; No. 43 (IX), Sept. 1970, pp. 27-28, Table lamp in African Blackwood studded with Ivory.

Berry, Louis. BSOT, No. 10 (II,5), Feb. 1954, p. 27. Polychromatic pin tray; No. 12 (III,2), Feb. 1955, p.31, Polychromatic table lamp; No. 14 (III,4) Feb. 1956. p.71, Inlaid plate; No. 24 (V) Feb. 1961, pp. 6-8. Method and example of studded and inlaid plaque of Sycamore, Yew, Tasua, Blackwood.

Borcherdt, Fred.in Meilach. q.v., p.68, Cylinder of laminated Maple and Walnut.

Bourne, William A. BSOT, No. 46 (X), Mar. 1972, p. 27, Inlaid lid.

Brasell, Austin L. BSOT, No. 40 (IX), Mar. 1969. p.143, Turned, laminated assemblies of native New Zealand woods.

Brown, Cyril. BSOT.No. 40 (VIII), Mar. 1969. pp. 143, 146-148; No. 44 (IX), Mar. 1971. p.1, Various polychromatic turning examples.

Brubaker, Jake. FWW, No. 7 (II,1), Summer 1977, p.65. Studded goblets and urns.

Cooper, A.H. BSOT, No. 45 (IX), Sept. 1971, p. 3. Sycamore plate with inlaid center.

Duffy, Thomas J. FWW, No. 14, Jan./Feb. 1979, p. 69. Bolection turning with inlaid bands; FWWDBII, p. 147. Fluted vase and bowl of Mahogany with bolection inlay.

East, George. BSOT, No. 24 (V), Feb. 1961, p. 25. No. 25 (V), Aug. 1961 p. 107, No. 26 (VI), Feb. 1962, p. 24. No. 30 (VI), Feb. 1964, pp. 127, 130, No. 38 (VIII), Mar. 1968, p. 83. No. 41 (IX), Sept. 1969, p. 160, Methods and apparatus for recessing inlay work.

Gilson, Giles. FWW, No. 29, July/Aug. 1981, p. 57, GTO, p. 18, Nish, ARTISTIC WOODTURNING, q.v., p. 217, Calendar jar, inlaid stave work of Mahogany, Curly Maple, Ash, Padouk, Amaranth, Rosewood, Ebony, Bubinga, Walnut and Satinwood; GTO, p. 19, Laminated bowl of Ash, Padouk and Ebony.

Grace, W.A. BSOT, No. 27 (VI), Aug. 1962 (suppl.), No. 24 (V), Feb 1961 (suppl.) Methods for inlay turning.

Griffiths, D. BSOT, No. 41. (IX), Sept. 1969, p. 159, Boxes and frames showing polychromatic work.

Gutzeit, Chris. FWWDBII, p. 142, Inlaid pedestal bowl.

Halcrow, J.M. BSOT, No. 54 (XI), Mar. 1976, p. 2, Walnut bowl with Scottish plaid polychromatic inlay.

Hall, Fran W. FWW, No. 29, July/Aug. 1981, pp. 56-57. Studded inlay turning.

Haythornthwaite, Frank. BSOT, No. 8 (II,3), Feb. 1953, p. 6, No. 9 (II,4), Aug. 1953, p. 4, No. 27 (VI), Aug. 1962, p.28, Inlaid tray of Rosewood, Ebony, Acacia, Padouk, Yew; No. 18 (IV,3), Feb. 1958, p. 39, No. 21 (V), Aug. 1959, p. 1, No. 33 (VII) Sept. 1965, p. 107, No. 40 (IX), Mar. 1969, p. 143, Inlaid bowls and trays.

Hoffman, Carl. BSOT, No. 26 (VI), Feb, 1962, p. 12, Polychromatic inlay turning.

"Holtzapffel Minimus". BSOT, No. 26 (VI), Feb. 1962, p. 13, No. 27 (VI), Aug. 1962, p.28, General method for inlay turning.

Howe, Fred J. BSOT, No. 16 (IV,1), Feb 1957, p. 3, Yew tray inlaid with iron stained Yew.

Hunt, Dennis. BSOT, No. 54 (XI), Mar. 1976, pp. 34-36, Method and example of marquetry and inlaid vase of Iroko, English Walnut, Sycamore, Australian Silkwood, Yew, Rosa Peroba and Lacewood.

Irwin, Harry. FWW, No. 13, Nov. 1978, pp. 48-49, Bowls of laminated blocks.

Kelly, A.H. BSOT, No. 26 (VI), Feb. 1962, p. 1, Bowl of inlaid Imbura; No. 25 (V), Aug. 1961, p. 94, Turned tray of parallel laminations.

Knox, Frank. BSOT, No. 48 (X), Mar. 1973, p. 94, No. 51 (XI), Sept. 1974, p. 45, Amaranth tazza inlaid with coffee-wood (Diva-Diva).

Lammers, J. Paul. FWWDBII, p. 150, Salad bowl set of inlaid bands.

Macaulay, J. BSOT, No. 33 (VII), Sept. 1965, pp. 135-138, Jig for clamping laminated, inlay and segmented work.

Nash, Gerald, C. FWWBDB, p. 55, Studded display pedestals in Birch.

Sloan, Roger. FWWBDB, p. 78, Walnut twig pot with Oak root.

Standen, O. D. BSOT, No. 57 (XII), Sept. 1977, p. 68. Inlaid platter.

Trout, Robert. In Meilach, q.v., p. 164, Bowls of Vermillion with Birch studded inlay, p. 174, Bowl of Teak with Bonduc inlay.

Wylde, ---. BSOT, No. 32 (VII), Mar. 1965, pp. 55, 92. Turned box of Myall and Olivewood with Acacia inlay.

------. BSOT, No. 44 (IX), Mar. 1971, p. 24. An example of slender turning with studding and other forms of polychromatic turning.

Books covering Studding, Inlaying and Laminating.

Audsley, George A. and Audsley, Berthold. THE ART OF POLYCHROMATIC AND DECORATIVE TURNING, Small, Maynard & Co., Boston, 1916, pp. 33-49. Geometric and circular studding.

Baker, Glen E. and Yeager, L. Doyle. WOODS AND WOODWORKING , Sams & Co., Indianapolis, 1975, p. 302, Through studding for polka-dot.

Barnard, John ed., AMATEUR WORK ILLUSTRATED, Vol. IV, Ward, Lock & Co., London, Nov. 1884-Oct., 1885, pp. 576-578. Sequential inlaying of concentric studs, eccentric inlay, by Loidis.

Holtzapffel, John J. PRINCIPLES AND PRACTICES OF HAND OR SIMPLE TURNING, Vol. IV, Holtzapffel & Co. , London 1879, repub. Dover New York, 1976, pp. 537-543, figs. 739-742. Inlay turning method.

Holtzapffel, John J. PRINCIPLES AND PRACTICES OF ORNAMENTAL OR COMPLEX TURNING, Vol. V Holtzapffel & Co., London, 1884. Repub. Dover, New York, 1973. pp. 234-241. Inlay turning methods.

Meilach, Dona Z. CONTEMPORARY ART WITH WOOD, Crown, New York, 1968, p. 68. Cylinder of laminated Maple and Walnut by Borcherdt, q.v., pp. 164, 174. Inlaid Bowls by Trout, q.v. p. 167, Method of peg inlay in bowls.

Nish, Dale L. ARTISTIC WOODTURNING, Brigham Young University Press, Provo UT. 1980. pp. 106-127. Methods of bowl decoration by studding.

Pinto, Edward H. TREEN AND OTHER WOODEN BYGONES, G. Bell & Sons, London, 1969. pp. 220, 310, pl. 233, 323. Studded, inlaid draughts set, lace bobbin decorated with studding.

Rebhorn, Eldon. WOODTURNING, McKnight & McKnight, Bloomington, Ill. 1970. pp. 68, 69, 104, 132. Methods and examples of vertical inlay bands in vases and cylinders.

BLOCKING, SINGLE AND MULTIPLE, INCLUDING CROSS LAMINATION.

Abell, S.G. BSOT, no. 7 (II,2), Aug. 1952, p. 25. Polychromatic work.

Barklow, John. FWW, No. 29, July/Aug. 1981, pp. 54-55. Geometric blocking and lamination in Walnut, Basswood and Maple.

Berry, Louis. BSOT, No. 10 (II,5), Feb. 1954, p. 27. Pin tray by blocking; No. 12(III,2), Feb. 1955, p. 31. Polychromatic table lamp.

Brody, Max. FWW, No. 3 (I,3), Summer 1976, p. 44. Gavels of alternating light and dark woods.

Cole, Janice and Kress, Warren. FWWDBII, p. 149. Stacked and blocked vase in six woods.

Darnell, Paul. FWW, No. 29, July/Aug. 1981, p. 52. Laminated, blocked vase, method.

Dennison, Dan. FWWDBII, p. 174. Blocked table lamp in Walnut, Bubinga and Zebrawood.

Fischman, Irving. FWW, No. 1 (I,1) Winter 1975, pp. 16-19, Cover FWWBDB, p. 89. Laminated and segmented bowl in Teak and Walnut.

Fowler, K.J. BSOT, No. 40 (IX), Mar. 1969, p. 150. Flat bottom bowl of stave work; No. 3 (I,3), Aug. 1950, p. 4, No. 11 (III,1), Aug. 1954, p. 5, No. 47 (X), Sept. 1972, p. 45. Polychromatic vase; No. 16 (IV,1), Feb. 1957, p. 1. Polychromatic bowls.

Fuller, --. BSOT, No. 16 (IV,1) Feb. 1957, p. 2. Polychromatic table lamp in multicolored plastics.

Hinckley, Edwin C. in Nish, CREATIVE WOODTURNING, q.v., pp. 221, 241. Laminated Walnut bowls.

Howe, Fred J. BSOT, No. 10 (II,5), Feb. 1954, p. 31. Barrel by circular layering and incutting.

Knox, Frank. BSOT, No. 39 (VIII) Sept. 1968, pp. 112-113. Table lamp of three checker blocked balls; No. 39 (VIII), Sept. 1968, p. 112, No. 51 (XI), Sept. 1974, p. 14. Calico bowl with checkerboard bottom in eleven woods.

Kravarik, William. FWWBDB, p. 82. Blocked tea cup and saucer.

Lutrick, David J. FWWBDB, p. 164, Blocked rolling pin in Walnut, Cherry, and Maple.

Lyons, Glen R. GTO, p. 46. Walking stick of laminated Ash and Rosewood.

Oldaker, Howard C. FWWBDB, p. 86. Blocked table lamp stand in Cypress and Walnut.

Osolnik, Rude. FWW, No. 1 (I,1), Winter, 1975. p. 14. Bowl of solid Birch plywood; GTO, p. 57. Bowl of laminated Mahogany and Birch plywood; in Nish ARTISTIC WOODTURNING, p. 239. Bowl of stacked veneers.

Pack, Ted. FWW, No. 29. July/Aug. 1981, pp. 52-54. Method and examples of spindle laminations: Sandwich, stack, multiple sandwich, checkerboard, and chevron.

Patrick, William. GTO, pp. 58-59, Plates of Zebra, Mahogany, Walnut, Curly Maple and Goncalo Alves; Nish, ARTISTIC WOODTURNING, q.v. p. 213, Plates as above.

Pearson, E.N. in Nish, CREATIVE WOODTURNING, q.v. p. 201. Table lamp of blocked woods, p. 214 Toothpick holder of blocked laminations.

Quinn, William E. FWW, No. 2 (I,2) Spring 1976, p. 6. Checkered bowls.

Rogers, James W. FWWDBII, p. 147. Compote of blocked Walnut, Ash and Maple.

Schneider, Richard. GTO, p. 70. Helicoid mosaic flat laminated bracelets.

Schuette, Lee A. FWW, No. 1 (I,1) Winter 1975, p. 14. Rolling pin of solid Birch plywood and Walnut.

Schwoch, Everett. FWWDBII, p. 173. Lectern stand of blocked Maple, Walnut, Oak and Birch.

Smith, John W. GTO p. 74. Lidded jar of laminated, blocked Rosewood and Ebony.

Trout, Robert G. in Nish, CREATIVE WOODTURNING, q.v., p. 223. Laminated Olivewood bowl.

Walstad, Dennis. FWWDBII, p. 146. Through laminated bowls of Walnut faced plywood

Warner, Dan. FWWDBII, p. 154. Blocked rolling pins of Cherry, Maple, Purpleheart and Angico.

-----. BSOT, No. 36 (VIII), Mar. 1967, p. 45, No. 40 (IX), Mar. 1969, p. 141 Deep bowl with mosaic bottom and inset mosaic sides.

Books covering Blocking, Single and Multiple, Including Cross Lamination

Audsley, George A. and Audsley, Berthold. THE ART OF POLYCHROMATIC AND DECORATIVE TURNING, Small, Maynard & Co., Boston, 1916, pp. 53-74, pl. 3,4,5. Blocking and lamination for spindle work, across and parallel to axis of turning. Methods.

Baker, Glen E. and Yeager, L. Doyle. WOODS AND WOODWORKING, Sams & Co., Indianapolis, 1975. pp. 302-303. Blocking method.

Blandford, Percy W. WOODTURNER'S BIBLE, Tab Books, Blue Ridge Summit PA. 1979. pp. 177-189. Methods for blocked bowls and platters.

Capotosto, Rosario. COMPLETE BOOK OF WOODWORKING, Pop. Sci. Harper & Row, New York, 1975. p. 12. Salt and Pepper set of turned, laminated veneers, pp. 220, 333. Method of stacked rings for turning, p. 332. Spindle turned blocking of contrasting woods.

De Cristoforo, R.J. BUILD YOUR OWN WOOD TOYS, GIFTS AND FURNITURE, Pop. Sci./Harper & Row, New York, 1979. Nut bowl of Multi-tier blocking.

Ensinger, Earl W. PROBLEMS IN ARTISTIC WOODTURNING, Woodcraft Supply Co. Woburn MA 1978. pp. 22-23. Methods and measurements for darning eggs in Cedar, Walnut, Mahogany, Maple and Magnolia.

Gunerman, Milton. SELECTED WOOD TURNING PROJECTS, Home Craftsman Publ., New York, 1952, pp. 13, 19, 20. Bowls from stacked blocks; pp. 73-75. Method for lamp stand with turned, laminated overlay of contrasting woods.

Nish, Dale L. ARTISTIC WOODTURNING, Brigham Young University Press, Provo, UT. 1980. pp. 72-81, 213.Multi-tierd blocked bowls. Methods.

Nish, Dale L. CREATIVE WOODTURNING, Brigham Young Univ. Press, Provo, UT. 1975. pp. 155-163. Laminated and blocked bowls. Methods. pp. 214, 221, 223, 240, 241. Blocked Lathework examples.

Pain, Frank. THE PRACTICAL WOODTURNER, Sterling Pub. New York. 1979. Ring napkins, studding, blocking, inlaying.

Pinto, Edward H. TREEN AND OTHER WOODEN BYGONES, G. Bell & Sons London, 1969. p. 310, pl. 323, Lace bobbins of stacked woods; p. 315 pl. 339, Needlecases of stacked woods.

Pinto, Edward H. TUNBRIDGE AND SCOTTISH SOUVENIR WOODWARE, G. Bell & Sons, London, 1970. pl. 11, 29. Turned stickware of blocked work.

Rebhorn, Eldon. WOODTURNING, McKnight & McKnight, Bloomington, IL. 1970. pp. 136-137. Vases of blocked woods with methods and dimensions.

Seale, Roland. PRACTICAL DESIGNS FOR WOOD TURNING, Evans Bros. London, 1964. Studded bowl together with other projects.

Stokes, Gordon. MODERN WOODTURNING, Sterling Pub. New York, 1979. Laminating, coopered work and segmenting.

Stokes, Gordon. WOODTURNING FOR PLEASURE, Prentice Hall. N.J. 1980. pp. 102-105. Section of coopered work. pp. 37-46.

Wille, M.W. ART IN WOOD , Bruce, Milwaukee, 1966. pp. 40-41. Method, material and measurements for table lamp by blocking.

SEGMENTING, RING AND SECTOR, STAVE WORK.

Brown, Emmett E. BSOT, No. 40 (IX) Mar. 1969. p. 143. Advanced forms of segmentation.

Chess, W.L. FWW, No. 28, May/June, 1981, p. 20. Method for clamping segments for gluing.

Davis, John G. FWWDBII, p. 151. Tray of curly maple segments.

Fischman, Irving. FWWDBII, p. 148. Staved bowl of Teak, Zebrawood, Walnut.

Graves, Garth F. FWW, No. 10, Spring 1978. pp. 70-72. Methods and examples of mugs, plates and bowls from stacked rings and staved assemblies.

Hartley, Steven H. FWW, No. 14, Jan/Feb 1979., pp. 61-65. Globe and stand turned from stave work.

Harwood, John R. FWW, No. 2 (I,2), Spring, 1976, pp. 5-6. Lamination methods for turning.

Hewitt, Robert. FWW, No. 10, Spring, 1978. p. 73. Method, jigs and calculations for compound-angled stave work, example glued up and turned.

Higbee, Peter. FWWDBII, p. 155. Rolling pin of stave construction. Maple, Walnut, and Cherry.

Hurwitz, Michael. FWWBDB, p. 79. Staved bowl.

Kelsey, John. FWW, No. 10. Spring, 1978, p. 73. Describes Hewitt's methods, q.v.

Lawrence, Pope. FWW, No. 25. Nov./Dec., 1980. p. 26. Method of assembly of staved cylinder.

Leeke, John. FWW, No. 28., May/June, 1981. p. 78. Coopered columns.

Macauley, J. BSOT, No. 33 (VII), Sept. 1965, pp. 135-138. Jig for clamping laminated, inlay and segmented work.

Miller, Geoff. FWW, No. 6 (I,6), Spring, 1977. p. 55. Ring Staved bowls.

Mortenson, Tom. FWWBDB, p. 78. Blocked and staved bowl of Koa and Walnut.

Nish, Randy. Nish. CREATIVE WOODTURNING, q.v., p. 210. Walnut bowl constructed of segmented rings.

Pratt, D.I. BSOT, No. 33 (VII), Sept. 1965, p.108. Vases of segmented work; No. 36 (VIII), March 1967, p.15. Bowls of laminated cylindrical ring segments.

Roccanova, Michael. FWWBDB, p. 80. Staved fruit/plant basket with herringbone inlay, Walnut and Basswod.

Saylan, Merryll. GTO, pp.65-66, Barbell, doughnut of turned segments of Maple, Poplar and acrylic.

Schulz, John W. GTO, p. 71. Bowl of laminated, staved construction.

Scheffield, Eric. FWWDBII, p. 160. Staved and laminated globe.

Tara, Jozef and Feely, Joseph. FWWBDB, p. 79. Stacked, laminated salad bowl set.

Trotman, Bob. FWWBDB, p.79. Staved bowl of Cherry and Walnut.

"Turner, A. Prentice". BSOT, No. 27 (VI), Aug. 1962, pp. 49-50, No. 24 (V), Feb. 1961, p. 2. Ring type segmented tankards.

Waterman, Asaph G. FWW, No. 10, Spring 1978, p. 74. Table saw and assembly jigs for stacked ring staved bowls.

Webb, Thomas. FWW, No. 10. Spring 1978, p. 75. Calculations for staved cones.

White, Bob. Nish. ARTISTIC WOODTURNING, q.v. p. 214. Walnut table lamp of segmented ring construction.

Books covering Segmenting, Ring and Sector, Stave Work.

Baker, Glen E. and Yeager, L. Doyle. WOODS AND WOODWORKING, Sams & Co. Indianapolis, 1975. p. 302. Method for layered segmented work for turning.

Blandford, Percy W. WOODTURNER'S BIBLE, Tab Books, Blue Ridge Summit, PA. 1979. pp. 180-186. 226-227, 374-376. Methods for assembling contrasting segments and turning them.

Capotosto, Rosario. COMPLETE BOOK OF WOODWORKING, Popular Science/ Harper Row. New York, 1975. pp. 231, 356. Miter and bevel angle settings for staved segments for 3 through 14 sides. (12 polygons)

Child, Peter. THE CRAFTSMAN WOODTURNER, G. Bell & Sons, 1976. London. pp. 214-221. Bowls of ringed segments and laminated layers.

Evan-Thomas, Owen. DOMESTIC UTENSILS OF WOOD, E.P. Publ. 1973. pp. 6-7. Walnut and Sycamore Scottish quaich; Staved and coopered bowls of the 18th century.

Nish, Dale L. ARTISTIC WOODTURNING, Brigham Young Univ. Press, Provo, UT. 1980. pp. 82-105, 214, 217. Methods and examples of bowls by segmenting.

Nish, Dale L. CREATIVE WOODTURNING, Brigham Young Univ Press, Provo, UT. 1975. pp. 148-154, 164-171, 210. Methods and examples of bowls by segmenting.

Pinto, Edward H. TREEN AND OTHER WOODEN BYGONES, G. Bell & Sons, London, 1969. pp. 53-54, Pl. 46, p. 142, Pl. 143. Scottish bickers and quaiches in staved Laburnam, box, Holly, Sycamore, dyed Alder, and Lignum Vitae; Staved salt box.

Slater, David. WOOD TURNING MADE EASY, Cassell & Co., London, 1957, pp. 49-57. Methods for staved and segmented work.

Stokes, Gordon. WOODTURNING FOR PLEASURE, Prentice Hall, New Jersey. 1980. pp. 37-46, 102-105. Covers coopered work.

Following is a supplemental bibliography covering Adhesives and Glues, important for the polychromatic turner.

Baker, Glen E. and Yeager, L. Dayle. WOODS AND WOODWORKING, Sams and Co. Indiamapolis, 1975. pp. 247-250.

Capotosto, Rosario. COMPLETE BOOK OF WOODWORKING, Popular Science/ Harper Row. New York. 1975. pp. 346-357.

Capron, J. Hugh. WOOD LAMINATING, McKnight & McKnight, Bloomington, Ill. 1963. pp. 29-34.

Coleman, Donald G. WOODWORKING FACTBOOK, Speller & Sons, New York, 1966. pp. 155-173.

Dahl, Alf and Wilson, J Douglas. CABINETMAKING AND MILLWORK, American Technical Society, Chicago. 1956. pp. 188-194.

Daniels, George. GLUES AND ADHESIVES, Popular Science/ Harper Row. New York. 1979. pp. 6-49, 69-78.

Feirer, John L. CABINETMAKING AND MILLWORK, Bennett Co. Peoria, Ill. 1970. pp. 533-551.

-110-

Forest Products Laboratory, U.S.D.A. WOOD HANDBOOK, U.S. Government Printing Office. 1955. pp. 233-245.

Hobbs, Harry J. VENEERING SIMPLIFIED, Scribner's Sons, New York. 1978. pp. 49-59.

Joyce, Ernest. THE ENCYCLOPEDIA OF FURNITURE MAKING, Sterling Publications. 1978. pp. 143-150.

Selbo, M.L. ADHESIVE BONDING OF WOOD, Sterling Publication, New York. 1978.

Following is a supplemental bibliography of books helpful to the turner in relation to wood types and description.

Audsley, George A. and Audsley, Berthold. THE ART OF POLYCHROMATIC AND DECORATIVE TURNING, Small, Maynard & Co. Boston, 1916. pp. 17-29.

Bridgwood, Alfred E. ed. NEWNES CARPENTRY AND JOINERY, Vol. I Newnes, Ltd, London. ND c. 1950. pp. 222-235.

Brough, J.C.S. TIMBERS FOR WOODWORK, Lippincott, Philadelphia, ND c. 1950. pp. 88-196.

Coleman, Donald G. WOODWORKING FACTBOOK, Speller & Sons, New York, 1966.

Constantine, Albert. KNOW YOUR WOODS, Rev. ed. Charles Scribner Sons, New York. 1975.

Core, Harold A. and Cote, Wilfred A. and Day, A.C. WOOD STRUCTURE AND IDENTIFICATION, Syracuse Univ. Press, Syracuse, New York. 1976.

Corkhill, Thomas. A GLOSSARY OF WOOD, Stobart & Son, London. 1979.

Dahl, Alf and Wilson, J. Douglas. CABINETMAKING AND MILLWORK, Amer. Tech. Soc. , Chicago, 1956. pp. 186-187, 199-203.

Edlin, Herbert L. WHAT WOOD IS THAT? Viking, New York. 1969.

Edlin, Herbert. L. THE ILLUSTRATED ENCYCLOPEDIA OF TREES, Harmony, New York. 1978.

Farmer, R. H. HANDBOOK OF HARDWOODS, 2nd ed. HMSO, London. 1972.

Feirer, John L. CABINETMAKING AND MILLWORK, Bennett Co. Peoria, Ill. 1970. pp. 80-116.

Forest Products Laboratories, Canada. CANADIAN WOODS, THEIR PROPERTIES AND USES, Canadian Resource and Development Dept. Ottawa, 1951.

Forest Products Laboratory, U.S.D.A. WOOD HANDBOOK, U. S. Government Printing Office.1955 and later editions.

Hobbs, Harry. J. VENEERING SIMPLIFIED, Scribner's Sons, New York. 1978.

International Wood Collectors Society. BULLETIN OF THE INTERNATIONAL WOOD COLLECTORS SOCIETY, Donald Smurthwaite, 632 S.E. 20th Court, Hillsboro, Oregon, 97123.

Kribs, David A. COMMERCIAL FOREIGN WOODS ON THE AMERICAN MARKET. Dover, New York, 1968.

Manager of Pulbications, India. INDIAN WOODS, Vols. I, II, III. Manager of Publications, Delhi, 1958, 1960, 1972.

Record, Samuel, IDENTIFICATION OF THE ECONOMIC WOODS OF THE UNITED STATES. Wiley. New York. 1919.

Record, Samuel and Robert Hess. TIMBERS OF THE NEW WORLD. Yale University Press. 1943. Arno Publ. 1972.

Record, Samuel and Clayton Mell. TIMBERS OF TROPICAL AMERICA. Yale University Press. 1924.

Timber Research and Development Association. TIMBERS OF THE WORLD, Vols. I, II. The Construction Press, Lancaster, England. and Longman Inc. New York, 1979, 1980.

INDEX